T0365989

HOPE:
What It Can Do

PASTOR OMOJEVWE BROWN EMMANUEL

 www.trafford.com

North America & international
toll-free: 844-688-6899 (USA & Canada)
fax: 812 355 4082

To my precious and adorable wife, Pastor (Mrs) Rose Omjevwe, for her unmovable faith and strong hope in God, also for her love and care for me and our children.

CONTENTS

ACKNOWLEDGEMENTS

Thanks to God Almighty for His unfailing love, grace, mercies, provisions, and protection upon my life, my wife, and children; also for His knowledge and wisdom upon me to bless the body of Christ with this wonderful book.

In addition, my special thanks go to my adorable and beautiful wife, the best life companion, and my wonderful, beautiful children, Divine and Joanna, for giving me reasons to write this book. God bless you, anoint you, and may His glory establish you in Jesus's name. Amen.

I must appreciate all members of our ministry in all the nations. I thank you all for your support, prayers, and mostly for believing in me as your spiritual leader.

God bless you in Jesus's name.

Finally, I thank everyone in our prayer group for their prayers. You are wonderful solders of Christ. I also thank those who made financial contributions and my gratitude to the publishing company for a good and well done job. No amount of words can be enough to express the joy of the Lord in my heart towards each of you.

I pray that this book will mightily bless the world, mostly the hopeless and helpless.

I hope this book will draw them near to God in Jesus's name.

Amen.

INTRODUCTION

Hope— What it can do. Our hope in God can do all things and will do everything we ever desired or think to achieve. Its power in our lives requires no augmentation or calculation. Hope simply means you can when it seems you cannot. Those who go for hope go for everything and get them achieved effortlessly.

It is spiritually unacceptable, unexplainable, and humanly difficult to live life without hope. Hope is our life, hope is our future, hope is our happiness, and our hope in God is the joy of the world.

This book will draw you near to God and win undecided souls to God's kingdom. Also, this book will point you to the importance of faith and hope in God alone.

No other sources of hope, apart from God, can save us or a nation from a day or year of trouble or pandemic like COVID-19.

There is no other way to receive miracles from God unless you have faith on His Son Jesus Christ and have full hope in His word, belief in His prophets, and trust in God. You must put your trust and hope in Him when your situation seems hopeless or worrisome.

Unwavering hope in the word of God moves God to perform what He promised us.

In my years in ministry work, as a prophet of God, I have seen a lot of unbelievable things and unholy confessions amongst some Christians. They often confessed with their mouth negative words that destroy their hope. Some of these words totally lack the wings of faith to fly us into a miracle, words like 'I am tired of everything', 'Why God has not answered my prayer? I have prayed all the prayers, yet God refused to heal or answer me', 'Is everything prayer, Pastor? I can't kill myself again'. Some even told me, 'Pastor, It is my destiny. So let me carry my cross'.

Listen to me. Stop negative confessions that kill your miracles. Who told you that problems are your destiny from God?

Don't believe or even accept such words or even imagine such in your heart.

Apply the power of the God's word in your spirit and do damage to every unpleasant situation of your life.

Where is your trust and hope in God? You can't be hopeless when you study your Bible. When you have Jesus Christ as your hope, God performs all He promised you.

The problem of some Christians is that once their miracle is delayed, they lose trust in God, and going to church becomes uninteresting. We lack patience and enduring grace to wait upon God; neither do such people show interest in praying to God again. I call them 'home worshippers' or 'self-made pastors'. They flip from one television channel to another, paying attention to seducing and corrupting headlines, while some people stationed their eyes on the television screen, watching favourite movies, games, or better still watching any television pastors from one channel to another to keep them busy.

In this book, I analysed reasons why you must put your hope in God and not on a man of God or on your educational qualifications.

Some people's problems are in their education. They analyse point by point their situations with classroom knowledge and conclude that their problem is not spiritual but psychological, emotional, or stress or normal because it can happen to anyone. Even when such people believe that their problem is spiritual and not medical or psychological, they cannot find a way to solve the problem. They hope on scientific test analysis and the judgmental world thinking about things that happened to mankind. These are things that are tormenting our hope in God.

Finally, such people will lose hope completely. That is why most educated people find it difficult to settle down in marriages because they never believed that demons or powers of darkness cannot stop them from getting married or meeting or achieving their goals in life.

There are no human problems that the powers of darkness do not get involved.

Never allow your education or overcivilisation or exposures to becloud your mind and blind your eyes to the extent of losing hope in God.

There are solutions to all problems of man, but it requires our total trust in God and His words.

Scientific knowledge and education have destroyed us through theories and hypothesis, thereby making us an enemy of the gospel, thereby hindering us from receiving a miracle from God.

Millions of people died from drug prescriptions that their personal physicians gave them. But your hope in God gives you a healthy and peaceful life.

Education is good, but don't allow it to destroy your faith and hope in God through Christ Jesus. To keep your relationship with God, you must first keep your hope in Him, then your relationship with Him will produce your heart's desires.

Apart from hope and trust in God, this book will also open the ears of the deaf, open the eyes of the blind. Those are the educated Christians who never see anything wrong about their lives. It will open the mind of those who are under the spell of darkness. I mean those who go to church but believed not or have no hope on the word of God.

Position your mind into positive thinking, and you will find reasons to tackle all your difficulties with the power of faith and hope in God.

Christians who thought that having hope in God is time wasting will discover from this book that they will actually save themselves from frustration, fake news, fake prophesy and fake preachers, palm readers, and evil seers they consult to solve their life problems.

Hope in God is what you need and what you need now! Stop complaining about your situation to mockery. I recommend this book for Christians who need miracles to end their pains. It will change you and give your life meaning.

Jesus Christ is my hope. what about you?

SOMETHING IS NOT RIGHT ANYMORE

Everything in life that you possess, like houses, cars, certificates or degrees, children, wife or husband, investments, and fame, will surely cause you hopelessness and frustration if you don't have Jesus Christ as your hope.

If you don't have Jesus Christ before acquiring wealth, you can never escape hopelessness and frustration in life. Everything man have in life outside God's provision makes man hopeless and gives man sleepless night.

But if you have Jesus Christ as your hope in life, everything He created, He will give you peace, joy, and happiness.

You cannot get hope from this world or from the things this world offers because the world people live now is full of satanic agents, and these agents cause wars between nations, manipulate the economy to their own interest, create deadly diseases and virus through evil laboratories to kill and to destroy the entire plan of God for man.

Things that make man hopeless that the devil created, and still creating, are increasing each day. Only those who have Jesus Christ as hope will survive the troubles this wicked world gives.

The priest, the pastor, and the most respected spiritual church leaders that the sheep look up to have disappointed man and God. These servants of God have soiled the priesthood office.

The church endorsed abortion laws that kill children even at eight months old, accept gay marriage and wed gay couples, that homosexuality is not a sin, also the recent pandemic – COVID-19. Vaccines were endorsed by church leaders. They were supposed to reject the evil manipulation and pray like Elijah who single-handedly disgraced the prophets of Baal.

The same famous church leaders and powerful monarchs danced to the tune of the politicians. None of them could stand up against the government. Daniel, in the Bible, prayed to God when a deadly decree was made that nobody should pray to any God for thirty days.

> **⁴Then the presidents and princes sought to find occasion against Daniel concerning the kingdom; but they could find none occasion nor fault; forasmuch as he was faithful, neither was there any error or fault found in him.**
>
> **⁵Then said these men, We shall not find any occasion against this Daniel, except we find it against him concerning the law of his God.**
>
> **⁶Then these presidents and princes assembled together to the king, and said thus unto him, King Darius, live for ever.**
>
> **⁷All the presidents of the kingdom, the governors, and the princes, the counsellors,**

and the captains, have consulted together to establish a royal statute, and to make a firm decree, that whosoever shall ask a petition of any God or man for thirty days, save of thee, O king, he shall be cast into the den of lions. (Daniel 6:4–7)

Daniel put his hope in God, and he did this:

¹⁰Now when Daniel knew that the writing was signed, he went into his house; and his windows being open in his chamber toward Jerusalem, he kneeled upon his knees three times a day, and prayed, and gave thanks before his God, as he did aforetime. (Daniel 6:10)

Every church in the world was commanded to close, and influential church leaders asked worshippers to stay home. These leaders went online, either through Zoom or YouTube, to cajole God. They collected bribes from certain countries' governments and closed down the house of the Almighty God. This is the worst sin our generation did against God.

¹Woe be unto the pastors that destroy and scatter the sheep of my pasture! saith the LORD.

²Therefore thus saith the LORD God of Israel against the pastors that feed my people; Ye have scattered my flock, and driven them away, and have not visited them: behold, I will visit upon you the evil of your doings, saith the LORD. (Jeremiah 23:1–2)

These most respected priests were the first people to take the vaccine, go on television showing themselves as an example of disobedience to God's word. They left the saints with no choice but to take the vaccine. Imagine if the government of the day asks everyone to take the mark of the beast, 666. These so-called world-famous priests rushed to take it and forced the congregation to do the same. It's written: By their fruits, you shall know them.

It's written:

Beware of false prophets, which come to you in sheep's clothing, but inwardly they are ravening wolves.

Ye shall know them by their fruits. Do men gather grapes of thorns, or figs of thistles?

Even so every good tree bringeth forth good fruit; but a corrupt tree bringeth forth evil fruit.

A good tree cannot bring forth evil fruit, neither can a corrupt tree bring forth good fruit.

Every tree that bringeth not forth good fruit is hewn down, and cast into the fire.

Wherefore by their fruits ye shall know them. Mathew 7: 15 – 20 (kJV)

This is ridiculous and absurd. They put the lives of innocent children of God in danger and helpless. Our spiritual leaders kill our hope in God for healing! Don't rely on any so-called world-famous spiritual church leader anymore, but put your hope in God and read your Bible to gain confidence and faith.

CHAPTER

Hope in God

HOPE:

- ❖ **HOLD**
- ❖ **ON TO**
- ❖ **PRAYER**
- ❖ **EVERY TIME**

Until your hope in God stands you out, you cannot stand out in this wicked world.

WHAT IS HOPE?

The very heart of Christianity is called hope. We can also say hope means hold on to prayer every time. Hope is the wall of

1

our Christian living. If the fence or wall that gives the house protection is cracked or broken, the house will struggle to resist external forces, so also hope. Hope is a wall that fenced our Christian life and keeps us safe from all external forces. Hope revives our strength to follow Him, no matter the troubles, persecutions, trials, or criticisms we face daily.

Hope is a Christian's daily prayer apron that you must have to make your life successful and protect you from serious situations or storms.

If you want to stand tall and strong in this wicked world, you must make hope your scaffold and stand on it confidently. Once you make hope your scaffold, storms will remain under the scaffold – hope and nothing will shake your faith.

You cannot survive in life without heart and blood. Hope is the heart and blood of Christianity. If you must survive all wickedness of this world, you must keep your hope in God at optimal level. Our hope in God makes the difference when our faith in His words is unshakable. A man of hope is a man of faith, and a man of faith is results-oriented.

Hope measures our faith in God. When you are suffering from pain or facing difficult challenges, no matter how hopeless the situation is, you must have a convincing hope in God.

Rejoicing in hope; patient in tribulation; continuing instant in prayer. (Romans 12:12)

There is no man with hope in God who did not rejoice. You must be patient with yourself and God during trials. All the devil and its agents want to see is that you are distracted from prayer.

When you are devoted in prayer in the midst of tribulations, the devil loses it all.

Don't look weakly in the face of problems or pains; let your hope in God generate the energy you need to pray and stand strong and victorious.

> **Be strong and let your heart take courage, all you who hope in the LORD. (Psalms 31:24)**

Having hope means being strong if you must take control of your life situations.

A courageous man who is full of hope in God decides the end of every unpleasant situation he finds himself in.

> **¹³There are those who rebel against the light, who do not know its ways or stay in its paths.**
>
> **¹⁴When daylight is gone, the murderer rises up, kills the poor and needy, and in the night steals forth like a thief. (Job 24:13–14)**

The devil and those who work for him rebel against the innocents in their early life, sometimes from the womb of their mother trying to stop their light from shining, pushing them out of God's way or path.

The devil and his workers work evil against the innocents when daylight is gone; the murderer rises, kills the hope of people, causing them to suffer all sort of things in life.

Everybody you can see around was created by God, and He gave us hope to live for Him and to live with Him forever. But something went wrong in the morning life of people. The devil murdered their morning glory through sins, and they eventually lost hope of recovery. Sin is a killer of hope and future. The devil, a specialist killer and thief, secretly lay ambush with sin in his hand to murder people's destiny and eventually cause the children of God to lose hope in God and in life. For this reason, every home and every parent must be born again and ensure that their home is God's home. It is difficult for the devil to destroy born-again destiny with sin.

Sin is the strong weapon the devil used to ruin the morning glory of people. Therefore parents should guard themselves and children against sin.

Sources of Hope:

    i.   Biblical sources of hope
   ii.   Universal sources of hope

BIBLICAL SOURCES OF HOPE

❖ Hope in God and in His Word

> **O Israel, hope in the LORD from this time forth and forever. (Psalms 131:3)**

Christians are only permitted to put their hope in God. No man who ever put hope in any other gods that did not get disappointed. A student who wants to enroll for higher school examination to qualify for university degree must trust the examination body that will conduct the entrance examination. Most importantly, he must have hope in the examination body that will grant him admission to study his desired course.

A Christian who wants to win all battles of life must enroll in the victory college, where champions graduate, must believe the examination body (house of God), put trust in the examiner (God), and finally trust His word to be able to pass all examination papers – temptations papers, sickness papers, and trials papers in A+ aggregates.

The grades you have from the final scripts that angles marked in heaven will determine your promotion to the next class – successes on earth.

> **I wait for the LORD, my soul does wait, and in His word do I hope. (Psalms 130:5)**

Psalms says, 'I wait for the Lord'; if you are sure of the source of your strength or power, whatever the source tells you to do, you will obey. The same in the church; you must wait on God and hope in His word to obtain His promises.

If you can wait on people's promises, you have no excuses to leave the house of God simply because His promises are yet to be fulfilled.

> **Yet those who wait for the LORD**
> **Will gain new strength;**
> **They will mount up with wings like eagles,**
> **They will run and not get tired,**
> **They will walk and not become weary.**
> **(Isaiah 40:31)**

We gain inward strength through our hope in God. One thing trials do is to kill our strength.

If we first lost the strength and courage to work a miracle out of an unpleasant situation, the hope of recovery will remain in pendulum. Our strength during trials did not come from our physical bone or the food we eat; it came from God Himself. That is why we never get weary. The secret of the race to get oneself free from the enemy requires running the race with God's strength. Those who refused to have God's strength as vital element to end well refused to win nothing in life.

Then you would trust, because there is hope; and you would look around and rest securely. (Job 11:18)

Hope in God means you can count on Him for everything, and everything is yours through Him. Your hope in God will fill your life with joy and peace of mind; there is no reason to worry about wickedness of this world.

To have results in life, you must first get pregnant of hope and give birth to hope. Hope is a spiritual energy booster that increases your chances of thunderous testimonies.

❖ Hope in Christ's Second Coming

The Second Coming of our Lord Jesus Christ gives us hope, no matter what the world made us to pass through. Christians hope in our Lord Jesus's Second Coming in recent years increases doubts in our minds because of the complexity of Christians' pains and unexplainable daily attacks from the devil. Can we have the confidence that God will finally bring about the triumph of good, no matter how badly we disappoint Him? Yes, we can trust Him for victory.

If so, His coming is inevitable, and we need not lose hope. The sufferings and pains of this world will lose their powers. No matter what, we should have hope on the good triumphs, the sufferings that God allowed us to endure on the path of serving Him. The sufferings will lose their meaning because God would have accomplished His purposes in us.

❖ Hope in God's Promises

> **²⁹He gives power to the weak, and to** *those who have* **no might He increases strength. ³⁰Even the youths shall faint and be weary, and the young men shall utterly fall, ³¹But those who wait on the** LORD **shall renew** *their* **strength; they shall mount up with wings like eagles, they shall run and not be weary. (Isaiah 40:29–31)**

The first thing that we must note is that the future of our generations is most risky and uncertain without faith in God's promises. The difficulties Christians face today can be traced to present evils the world is using to weaken our faith in God.

Christians can be serene in the confidence that someday God will wipe out all evil. After all, our God is all-powerful and needs only to assume full control of the world to make it conform to His will.

The world we live in today and the world the next generation will live could possibly generate into near chaos. There can be no metaphysical guarantee against such a catastrophe. But there is a strong pragmatic ground for hoping in God's promises.

If the Christians can hold on to God's words and grow their hope on His powers, the human experiment to destroy the world will fail.

All the devil is doing is to weaken our faith, destroy our hope in God, and make mankind believe science and theories. These threaten our generation on every side, particularly in terms of nuclear annihilation or ecological suicide. All we need in the face of these dangers is our confidence in the power of God to sustain us Christians.

The forces of evil in high places from different countries have conspired to make Jesus Christ irrelevant, and the gospel, against sins or evil practices, must not be preached in any nation but that everyone must accept scientists' reports. Christians' only hope is Christ's resurrection, and we can reasonably put our trust and hope in God for our future, no matter what the world forcefully impose on us.

❖ Hope on His Justification by Faith

Through whom also we have obtained our introduction by faith into this grace in which we stand; and we exult in hope of the glory of God. (Romans 5:2)

The coming of His faith into our lives justified us and made us fix our hope on the works of justification He did for us. Christ's faith in us is the ground for our hope in God, and we are not bothered what the world is plotting against our faith.

You must have hope on what Jesus Christ has done for you on the cross of Calvary, for your future to remains bright. Your understanding of His works on the cross will take fear from you and fix hope into you.

Now may the God of hope fill you with all joy and peace in believing, so that you will

abound in hope by the power of the Holy Spirit. (Romans 15:13)

A justified man, through faith in Christ, finds joy and peace abundantly. There is no continuous winning without continuous living by His hope. Hope is the water that fills your empty life when tough situations dried up every chances of making it again. The good news here is that hope pedals you into glorious celebration after dark nights.

UNIVERSAL SOURCES OF HOPE

❖ Hope in Personal Good Job

People feel hopeful, happy, and comfortable when they have a good job that gives them all they want in life. Such people put hope on the job.

They will work with all their strength to reach the top position. The better the job you secured, the higher your hope of making to the top. Because they've landed a fulfilling, juicy job, when people in this category lose their job or the company winds up, they get frustrated and can hardly withstand the storms that follow next— the family's needs.

❖ Hope in Family Good Name

Everybody wants to be identified with a family with a good reputation, good political record, royal statues, or influence in the society, a family with huge investments and assets; everyone wants to do business with such family, everyone wants to marry from the family with a good name. People put hope in such people, and they can do anything to belong to the family because they feel that their future could change by being identified with the family. You can never deny that family name or reputation is crucial in our present society. In Christianity, people want to attend churches with big names; either the pastor preaches well or encourages sins or seductive dresses. It does not matter to them.

It does not matter to them. They just want to identify themselves with churches with big names. Their hope is in the man of God, either to get a job or get married quickly. They don't care about the choice of life such churches offer them. Some people attend big churches for personal interest, and once they achieved the purpose, they stop going to the church. Only the hopeful in God remains in the church, regardless of what the pastor preaches or does. It's not their business. But serving God is.

❖ Hope in Yourself—Sense of Well-Being

This comes from finding a meaningful way of spending your time with people you put hope on. You can have a holiday with such people. Praying in the mountain during a holiday makes no sense to them, but they go on grooving, partying, or hanging around the shopping mall for ice creams. This is not sin, per se, but when you put your hope on what makes you feel nice or good just for a moment, it's really worrisome.

❖ Hope in Our Wealth

Riches is a stranger, and no matter how wise or careful one may be in terms of spending, riches don't last forever without God's wisdom.

Wealth can only give you temporary satisfaction, but really, life satisfaction is in Christ Jesus. You can build your hope on temporary things. But build permanent hope on things that only God offers. Money is just a means of buying and selling, while hope is a means of receiving miracles and doing miracles through Jesus Christ. Wealth can never give you salvation, but Jesus Christ gives wealth and salvation. Think about it. In every ungodly wealth or ill-gotten wealth, there is a price to pay.

In today's world, where integrity and honesty are not relevant even in the house of God, people don't mind the dire consequences of what they do to make money.

Some Christians have joined the squad of 'I must make by force'.

They make money and lose their conscience; society allows people with ill-gotten wealth to rule. They use money to rig election votes or supply guns to kill or harass their political opponents. These set of people are everywhere, in every nation, operating in different ways, as political monsters or oppressors or spiritual fraudsters, as in case of church leaders.

They put hope on their wealth. They break laws, and nobody dare challenge them. They made themselves untouchable, and the society honours them with medal awards.

When you put hope on your wealth, you have destroyed yourself completely.

❖ Hope in our certificates or degrees

Do you know that some educated people who are born again faced tough problems either in their marriage, health or other areas of life. Some professors believed that with their wells of knowledge they are secured in life. So going to church to listen to primary school dropped out with bad English, is an insult on their personality. They put hope on their educational qualifications and never thought it wise to trust God. Listen to me, I have seen a medical doctor whose wife died of cancer and he could not save his wife. Also I have seen a man of God whose wife was diagnosed of cancer and she was healed miraculously. With what is happening now in the world, our professors of medicine and best scientists has failed us. Non of them could provide solution to covid – 19 but rather they turn the situation to make money for themselves.

You can never defeat the devil with your educational qualification status but with word's of God you can. Put your degrees on the table and command your problems to hear your degrees and disappear. impossible! But you can put your bible on the table and decree that His word should act now by faith, surely your problem will hear the voice of His word and will immediately disappear. praise God!

It's written:

> [19] For the wisdom of this world is foolishness with God. For it is written, "He catches the wise in their *own* craftiness"; 1 Corinthians 3:19 (NKJV)

Also

> [5] Trust in the LORD with all your heart,
> And lean not on your own understanding;
>
> [6] In all your ways acknowledge Him,
> And He shall [a]direct your paths.

Proverbs 3:5-6 (NKJV)

All your university degrees / knowledge put together can not be compared with the knowledge of Satan; remember that the devil was in the garden of Eden before man and even before universities were created. You can't study problems or demons off your life. The Bible knowledge is the only knowledge the devil bow down for; therefore rely on the word of God.

Today's society is getting worse by the day, and it will continue to get worse till the coming of our Lord Jesus Christ.

Nowadays, nobody wants to attend a church where the pastor preaches against immoralities, seductive dressing, and repentance. What people are interested to hear is prosperity sermons, messages that encourage people to do the will of the flesh.

Some church congregations put their faith and hope on the man of God.

Worshippers hunt for wealthy men of God who will not mention their sins on the pulpit but encourage them to sin more. They are not worried about the deceiving messages of men of God, but his money is the message they are interested in.

You cannot serve mammon and God together. Those who serve God because they want to be super rich will sure fall into the trap of blood money or scams. The end of such people is supper poor after the devil is done with them.

HOPE IN PERSONAL WEALTH LEADS TO DISTRACTION FROM GOD'S PROTECTION AND QUICK DEATH.

HOPE IN PEOPLE LEADS TO DISAPPOINTMENT AND ABANDONMENT.

HOPE IN YOURSELF OR YOUR ABILITY LEADS TO CONFUSION AND SORROW.

HOPE IN CHRIST JESUS LEADS TO DELIVERANCE AND SALVATION.

Hope is the door that Christians use to enter into God's kingdom blessings. The day you have a permanent hope on the Lord Jesus Christ will be the end of all your worries about life achievements.

THINGS THAT KILL OUR HOPE

❖ Persistent problems

Persistent problems require persistent hope in God. It is true that persistent illness or problem can kill your hope in God. But as a Christian, your illness or problem is supposed to give you hope in God, not the other way round. The Bible talked about a woman with the issue of blood for twelve years. In Matthew 9:20–22, her sickness is supposed to kill her hope and faith in God, but she was cured with the utmost rapidity. When you have no faith in God, it will be difficult for you to believe Him for healing. There are a lot of people who have years of certain problem, yet they serve God and never stop going to church or attending church activities for once.

These people have unmovable faith in God. They have hope that one day God will heal them. When your illness refuses to go, be persistent in prayer for healing and in your services to God. Your hope in Christ Jesus for healing will come to pass if you are persistent in faith and hope.

❖ Lack of faith in the word of God

Since hope increases our faith, we need faith to increase our hope on the word of God. Hope comes by hoping on the word of God 'til the end. Christians need unmovable faith to make their hope stronger. Lack of faith in God's word kills our hope. In the absence of faith, there is nothing hope can do; faith is an essential force that elevates our hope, no matter the situation.

Don't just read the word of God without understanding. In your reading, get hope out of the word you read. When carefully read, with understanding, the words are with hope. Faith is a mixture of hope and results; stop gambling with your life. When you are just going to church without faith in God, you have killed your only hope of deliverance.

A lot of people nowadays go to the church because the man of God preaches well, with good English, or the church has the best architectural designs, or the man of God is very rich.

Today's youth are not bothered about faith or hope in God's word. Majority of them go to church when they are looking for future partners to date. To them, church is a social gathering, and every Sunday people gathered to show off. Even some pastors never see anything wrong with sins that today's youth commit.

The easiest way to go astray in life and lose the path of good ending is to count faith and hope in God not important.

The word of God will not work for you without faith and hope. Never you be deceived that Jesus has died for you, and no other works is required from you again. The truth is that Jesus died for us, but we must read the Bible, understand it, apply its principles to our lives, and have unshakeable faith in God. Hope is the access key to a glorious life. Don't kill yours.

❖ Lack of patience and endurance

Only those who has graduated with honourable degree in patience and endurance from the faculty trials conquer tough situation. When you lack this degree, you can never have hope in trials or worse situations.

If you want to see hope results in your life, seed of patience and endurance must grow in you.

Lack of endurance and patience has destroyed millions of people's hope. You can never harvest hope until patience becomes blood in your vein that f lows and endurance, the air you breathe.

Where are you hurrying to in life? You can't run faster than your shadow as your tongue cannot be faster than the words that come out of your mouth.

Too much of hurry has killed our faith and hope in God. You want everything fast and then live short years and die fast.

The rate of people dying at forty years is high because to them, to live a longer life is time wasting. They prefer to get rich overnight by hook or crook and live for only ten years and die.

Be patient with God. Is life not more than money and food? If you want quick success without waiting for God's time, you can never be faithful in your worship.

The rate of life accident amongst youth is higher on the fast lane – quick money.

Don't you know people have accidents in life, like premature death, marriage disasters, life injuries, and long suffering. There are no physical accidents without injuries.

So also is spiritual accident. Some People get injured their lives physically and spiritually because they can't wait for God's time. Road accident is majorly caused by lack of patience and endurance of road obstructions. Waiting on God's time is the cure to all life injuries.

❖ Unbelievers can kill a believer's hope

Having people who are not adding hope to your life is like tying yourself around with death. They will keep you hopeless for decades. Do you know that you do not actually need everyone who comes around you?

Unbelievers that some Christians keep as friends because they grew up in the same street or went to the same school destroy you with evil communications that you cannot resist.

Select people you want around you and, occasionally, examine their spiritual and physical contributions to your life.

Unbeliever, either it's your family or spouse or friends has the power to kill your hope in God.

When you tell them what is happening to you, they will feel it as flesh and see the situation as normal because they lack spiritual eyes and faith. They will show concerns, and within a period, they would have succeeded in wining your mind and will suggest alternatives ways of solving the problem, which is totally out of God's word.

Your hope on His word will die completely. Not all suggestions from people require your approval, mostly from an unbeliever.

Some Christians because of pressure from parents or friends, get married to unbelievers, believing that after the marriage, they will convert the unbeliever partner to God. Listen to me, you cannot convert any soul to God. It's the work of the Holy Spirit to covert people to God. We can only preach the gospel of Jesus Christ to people.

❖ Worldly desires and possessions

The rate at which some Christians are running after worldly things is on the increase.

You, as a child of God, must have zero appetites for riches and worldly possessions that can take you to hell fire.

In some churches, the message of prosperity and worldly possessions has destroyed the sheep faith and hope in God for genuine riches. Christians are great scammers now because their pastor is a chief scammer. It's shocking to hear some famous men of God using the pulpit of God to brag about their ill-gotten wealth. Pastor are not called to possess great wealth but are called to stand against the plans of the devil; that include sudden wealth through cocaine, stealing or robbery, blood money and internet fraudsters and human trafficking. All these are trap of the devil to destroy our hope in God for a peaceful life.

It is written: '**²¹Jesus said unto him, If thou wilt be perfect, go and sell that thou hast, and give to the poor, and thou shalt have treasure in heaven: and come and follow me.**

²²But when the young man heard that saying, he went away sorrowful: for he had great possessions.

²³Then said Jesus unto his disciples, Verily I say unto you, that a rich man shall hardly enter into the kingdom of heaven.

²⁴And again I say unto you, It is easier for a camel to go through the eye of a needle, than for a rich man to enter into the kingdom of God'. Mathew

The road to sudden wealth is the Broadway; only the greedy drive on it.

Don't misunderstand me. The children of God are not created to be poor, but you are not permitted to be super rich by do-or-die ways.

Thus says the LORD, your Redeemer, the Holy One of Israel:

'I *am* the LORD your God, who teaches you to profit, who leads you by the way you should go'. (Isaiah 47:17)

Isaiah's words in the above passage were an encouragement to the people of Israel who were suffering afflictions during their Babylonian captivity.

The same Holy Spirit is still speaking to us and gently leads the body of Christ through the peaks and pitfalls of this worldly corrupt systems.

He is the One who promised to teach Israel those things that would benefit them in this life and in the world to come.

It means our prosperous life was in God's own plan. This kind of prosperity means no lack but contentment.

Our present society celebrates the worst people in the society who got wealth in unquestionable ways, and the people in the environment knew that they are criminals, yet the society celebrate such people and honours them with federal government medal or global noble prize awards.

Excellence is often not given attention. You, as a believer living to obtain good reputations and thinking the society will value you, instead of you celebrated, those who have questionable wealth and possessions are made kings and rulers over you.

A man of worldly desires and possessions will influence you negatively, and if you buy into his evil deeds, your hope to making it in God's time will be killed.

❖ Our marriage partners can kill our hope

A good example is Job's wife in the Bible.

> **9. Then said his wife unto him, dost thou still retain thine integrity? Curse God, and die.**

> **10. Then said unto her, Thou speaketh as one of the foolish women speaketh, what?**

Shall we receive good at hand of God, and shall we not receive evil? In all this did not Job sin with his lips. (Job 2:9–10)

What a faithful man Job is. In the midst of serious trials, he has the right word to speak to his wife. Hope was so strong in his voice.

When you curse God in the midst of trials, you are a devil celebrant, and your chance of miracle is lost.

It's a suicide mission to marry a man or woman because of wealth, beauty, or family background. If either of the couple is not a born again, the other born again hope in God will be daily threatened. Your unbeliever wife or husband can kill your hope of serving God.

I have seen a situation where a man told his wife to chose between him and God; the woman called and said, 'I don't want my marriage to break pastor'. I said, 'Chose one out of the two'.

She stopped coming to our church and followed her husband. After some years, the man worked out of the marriage. The woman called me, and she said, 'Pastor, I have divorced that wicked man that called himself my husband'.

I allowed her to finish calling the man names, and I said, 'Madam, you cause it all.

If you stayed with God, your marriage issues would have been handled by God, and the man would have given his life to Christ through your endurance and faith in Christ. The woman's hope was washed away like an erosion by the husband 's marriage conditions. In any marriage that God is not totally respected, the marriage will not survive divorce.

The woman's hope was washed away like an erosion.

To call me for counseling was a difficult task. How could you allow marriage to separate you from God's church? These are people who never thought it wise to marry a Christian. They were after time, and pressure to get marry. 'I need a man to marry', 'I am getting old, and I just need a man'; or the man is cute and good-looking, and after all, he has a good job. 'I think he's a perfect choice'.

There' s no perfect time to marry and there's no perfect age to marry, once you are an adult you can marry at anytime. Therefore marring in an hurry to catch up with time is risky because the devil knows the state of your mind so he prepare a partner that will take you from God.

❖ Natural disasters

In the face of natural disasters, if not well handled with faith in God's word, you can lose all hopes completely, and it will affect your relationship with God.

Read Job 1:13–19, and you will get questions like 'Where was God when this happened to me?' 'Did I pray enough, or did I not obey his word?'

God has forgotten me. I am tired of going to church, and the pastor did not have anointing at all – fake pastor who cannot see vision, etc.

In the case of Job, he did not sin against God with his lips or did he charge God for his disasters.

Natural disasters kill hope the moment you start to use your mouth to curse God because of what happened to you. Instead of complicating things for yourself, go into fasting and prayer and allow God to heal your wounds. Also, seek for spiritual counselling from your pastor.

❖ Tough health challenges

When you are faced with health challenges and you have done everything humanly possible yet it seems your health is getting worse, your hope on God's words or prophesy will not be strong. The woman with blood issue in the Bible approached physicians and men of God for help, but none of them could give her hope of healing. Rather, they milked her pocket dry. But she didn't allow her health challenges to stop her from looking for Christ. Eventually, not only did she get healed, but she also received salvation.

Don't run away from God because He has not answered your prayers. Don't put all your hope on medical doctors when you have health challenges, the doctor could be used by the devil to kill for him. Doctors are human and they make mistakes in the theatre during operation. But if you put your hope in God for healing, He will use the best doctor for you. Don't run away from the house of God but run to His house for your healing.

It's written:

> Blessed is he who comes in the name of the LORD. From the house of the LORD we bless you. psalm 118:26 healing or good health is a blessing from God. When you have a strange sickness that defied medical solutions and your doctor keep telling that your test results are

perfectly fine. Deep down in your heart, your health is getting worst by the day, go to the altar of God and ask for healing. Not all Doctors knows that some sickness are arrow from the devil. The doctor that treat spiritual sickness of patients with injection or ant-biotic drugs will end up killing the patient because their sickness is an arrow from powers of darkness.

❖ Lack of total surrender to Jesus Christ

When your life is not fully dedicated to Jesus Christ or you are not ready to follow the narrow way, your hope in God will be dangling and your faith, unstable.

You must surrender your life to Jesus Christ and put your hope on Him.

He is capable of handling your life challenges and he will give you peace of mind.

Those who never see the need of total surrender to Jesus Christ will get their hope dashed.

A lot of so-called Christians belong to secret cult organizations and still attend church services. They are servers of two masters. Darkness and light have nothing in common. Either you serve God totally or you keep to your secrets cults.

For those who refused to submit their lives to Jesus Christ will surely have their hope dashed or lost completely.

BENEFITS OF HOPE IN GOD

❖ Hope Supply All Our Needs.

> **⁷Blessed is the man that trusteth in the LORD, and whose hope the LORD is.**
>
> **⁸For he shall be as a tree planted by the waters, and that spreadeth out her roots by the river, and shall not see when heat cometh, but her leaf shall be green; and shall not be careful in the year of drought, neither shall cease from yielding fruit. (Jeremiah 17:7–8)**

You cannot peacefully enjoy a successful life without sorrow unless your hope in Him makes you successful and grants you the peace that comes from Him, the King of Peace. Life without hope in Jesus Christ will always marry sorrows.

The Bible said, 'Blessed is the man that trust in the Lord and whose hope the Lord is. Your blessings start the day you make the Lord your trust and your hope. You will never experience drought; neither will you cease yielding fruits because your root of successful life is connected to his living waters – Jesus Christ.

The reason we fail in life is that we fail to have hope on God before we embark on the journey of life.

❖ Hope Increases Our Faith in God's Words.

Faith is the bedrock of Christianity, but our hope supplies fuel to our faith to follow Jesus Christ to the end, no matter what happens.

It's written :

> Now faith is the [a]substance of things hoped for, the [b]evidence of things not seen. ² For by it the elders obtained a good testimony. ³ By faith we understand that the [c]worlds were framed by the word of God, so that the things which are seen were not made of things which are visible.

Hebrews 11: 1-3 (NKJV)

The above Bible verses clearly tells us that hope and faith are closely intertwined. Without faith, we cannot increase in hope, and without hope, faith will be brought to standstill in our Christian lives. The greatest believers are those who put all their hope and trust on God.

Faith will tell you to choose suffering and afflictions than enjoy the passing pleasures of sins. This will in return add more sorrows.

Hope is resisting passing pleasures sin offers and receiving something better, made apart for us by God.

Since the word of God is our feet and vehicle that carries us to places, it means we need hope in His word to keep going. When you hope on His words, faith to follow will always be there. It is our hope on His words and promises that trigger our faith to follow Him.

Instances of people who have hope and faith at the dawn of history.

It's written:

> [4] By faith Abel offered to God a more excellent sacrifice than Cain, through which he obtained witness that he was righteous, God testifying of his gifts; and through it he being dead still speaks.

> [5] By faith Enoch was taken away so that he did not see death, "and was not found, because God had taken him"; for before he was taken he had this testimony, that he pleased God. [6] But without faith it is impossible to please Him, for he who comes to God must believe that He is, and that He is a rewarder of those who diligently seek Him.

> [7] By faith Noah, being divinely warned of things not yet seen, moved with godly fear, prepared an ark for the saving of his household, by which he condemned the world and became heir of the righteousness which is according to faith.

> Hebrews 11: 4-7 (NKJV)

Abel , Enoch and Noah are heroes of faith and fathers of hope. They have hope in the word of God from the dawn of their lives and were moved by faith to do more for God. When offer a sacrifice to God with hope that He will increase your harvest, your faith to give Him the best sacrifices will be developed. Christians must have hope at the dawn of the morning, and follow God with full hope on Him. Then obeying His words during trials wouldn't be difficult.

Since the word of God is our feet and vehicle that carries us to places, it means we need hope to keep going. When you hope on His words, faith to follow will always be there. It is our hope on His words and promises that trigger our faith to follow Him.

❖ Hope Energises Our Destiny.

The strength we need in life to face the future comes from our hope in Him.

When you have hope, you don't lack positive thinking. Hope gives you the energy to overcome trials. To feel weak in strength during trials means your hope has dropped, and to have victory may be difficult. Hope adds energy to us when we are weak in strengths and helps us win effortlessly. Hope sterilises our destiny that problems have destroyed and sharpens it again, turns it into a brand new destiny.

There is no powerful energy booster than hope. Hope boosts our future, provides us the strength to focus on our goals. It is the energy you need to light your future.

❖ Hope Lightens Our Darkness.

Hope recognises the presence of darkness but never worries about its existence.

Hope does not deny nor remove the reality of the dark—pains or afflictions.

One major attribute of hope is that in the midst of darkness, hope shines a bright light into our trials or valleys. With hope, you can see the end of everything from the beginning.

❖ Hope Heals Quicker.

I have had opportunities to meet with people with hopeless situations. They are really depressed. What I usually do is to get them near to myself and to the word of God.

I must tell you it's not easy to convince people with depression; sometimes my emotions make me to cry openly with them, seeing the pains and sufferings they are going through.

But I noticed that taking them as they are, getting near to them, heals them faster.

Once they hear the word of God with little prayers, miracles take place.

When you give people hope, they heal faster. However, when you discriminate people because of their hopeless situation, you kill their little hope, and they die shortly.

Depression is a sign of hopelessness. The situation will never and can never get better. That's why I often give testimonies about myself as an example to people whose situations seem helpless.

God has used me to put smiles on their face, to the glory of his Son Jesus Christ.

If I notice that they turned to me to hear what I am going to say, simple words like 'You will get better' or 'There is a way out', I knew that God has stepped in for them and that God is ready to wipe away their tears.

If I noticed that the person is crying and ready for prayer, I will make them profess that Jesus is their Lord and Saviour. Then I will pray with that person, and the healing starts.

Sometimes I give them transport money to return home. Our Lord is a healer and compassionate. He needs you to show care and love to the people with critical situation.

Within few weeks, testimonies of healing start to pour in.

❖ Hope Commands Storms to Be Still.

It's written:

> 23 And when he was entered into a ship, his disciples followed him. 24 And, behold, there arose a great tempest in the sea, insomuch that the ship was covered with the waves: but he was asleep. 25 And his disciples came to him, and awoke him, saying, Lord, save us: we perish. 26 And he saith unto them, Why are ye fearful, O ye of little faith? Then he arose, and rebuked the winds and the sea; and there was a great calm. 27 But the men marvelled, saying, What manner of man is this, that even the winds and the sea obey him! Matthew 8:23-27 (KJV) Jesus Christ was their Hope and the storm obeyed Him immediately.

It's written:

> He maketh the storm a calm, so that the waves thereof are still.
> Psalms 107:29 (KJV)

It's the storm (sins, curses or evil powers) that produces the wave — (sickness, failure, joblessness, late marriage, childlessness, confusion). there's no wave without a storm. Sometimes we caused the storms of our life and when the wave comes, we blame God and people around us for our problems. Our LORD Jesus Christ, He is a storm killer and wave calmer. Therefore, in the name of Jesus Christ, I command the storms of your life dead and it's wave still. Praise God!

Our present modern world that we live in is scientific, full of uncertainties and storms. Since we are still living in this world that is revolving around problems, where people are introduced to virus infections, hardship, and storms, we cannot totally rule out temptations and attacks. Even demons are part of the storms we face today. The activities of demons are spreading, and people in political powers are heavenly possessed with wicked demons.

In the midst of terrible and horrible storms of life, you must anchor on God's hope to fulfill your goals on earth.

Christians must have hope as anchor during troubled days. It's your hope in God's promises that will command the storm you are going through to be still.

You need not wait for dark days before you cast out your anchor of hope on God's saving power.

If you have Jesus Christ in your life, anytime storms arise against you, you can call upon your hope — Jesus Christ; and he will answer. Hope stabilises your faith during trials. Faith is not in enough when passing through troubles. You must have hope that at the end of the storm, wonderful testimonies will end it.

Finally, child of God, be strong and never fear your sorrowful situation for: God is our sure helper.

It's written:

> 17 The righteous cry, and the LORD heareth, and delivereth them out of all their troubles.
>
> 18 The LORD is nigh unto them that are of a broken heart; and saveth such as be of a contrite spirit.
>
> 19 Many are the afflictions of the righteous: but the LORD delivereth him out of them all.
>
> 20 He keepeth all his bones: not one of them is broken.
>
> Psalms 34:17-20 (KJV)

HOW CAN CHRISTIANS HAVE HOPE WHEN EVERYTHING LOOKS HOPELESS?

God's promises give hope to those who believe His Son Jesus Christ. Christians are not hopeless and must not allow any situation of their life end hopeless, but they must see the devil as the most hopeless and frustrated. There is no goal-getter who will spend time troubling other people or causing problem in the town; only a hopeless person goes about creating noise of nuisances.

Be proud of your faith and don't stop celebrating your God in your storms. The devil always gets sick when hearing people celebrating God in their troubles.

If everything looks hopeless, let your hope look strong against the storm.

> **Now the God of hope fill you with all joy and peace in believing, that ye may abound in hope, through the power of the Holy Ghost. (Romans 15:13)**

> **³And not only so, but we glory in tribulations also; knowing that tribulation worketh patience;**

> **⁴And patience, experience, and experience, hope:**

> **⁵And hope maketh not ashamed, because the love of God is shed abroad in our hearth by the Holy Ghost which is given unto us. (Romans 5:3–5)**

There is hope for everyone who truly believe in God. He will fill your heart with joy. The secret is that the devil never troubles any person who is not special in this world. The devil is afraid to withstand your blessings and the glory of God upon you, so he shakes your heart to fear him and brings storms to you so that you can surrender to his tricks. The only weapon against tribulations is hope in God.

OUR CHALLENGES AS CHRISTIANS CAUSE US TO

❖ Rely on God's words.

It's written:

> 1 He that dwelleth in the secret place of the most High shall abide under the shadow of the Almighty.
>
> 2 I will say of the LORD, He is my refuge and my fortress: my God; in him will I trust.
>
> 3 Surely he shall deliver thee from the snare of the fowler, and from the noisome pestilence.
>
> 4 He shall cover thee with his feathers, and under his wings shalt thou trust: his truth shall be thy shield and buckler.
>
> 5 Thou shalt not be afraid for the terror by night; nor for the arrow that flieth by day;
>
> 6 Nor for the pestilence that walketh in darkness; nor for the destruction that wasteth at noonday.
>
> 7 A thousand shall fall at thy side, and ten thousand at thy right hand; but it shall not come nigh thee.
>
> Psalms 91:1-7(KJV)

The entrance of God words into our heart during hopeless situations relieves us from depression. The word of God has the power to comfort us through the ministration of the Holy Spirit.

Rejoicing during hopeless situation does not mean that you are not a serious fellow. But it does mean that we can believe that God is doing a redemption work on the situation.

God does not disappoint or hurt us during such trying times. He builds our hope and faith and shapes us into His perfect plans.

When you read the word of God, you need no man to preach hope to you. No other book you may read during storms of tribulation or trouble that can give you hope.

The word of God will give you hope and inner strength to compel you to pray. If you read love books during trouble or storms, you have worsened the situation – demons like marine husband or wife or sexual demons will rape you while you are asleep.

Those who watch home movies or follow friends to cinema to cool off during tribulation are victims of unwanted pregnancy and drunkenness.

❖ Rely on God's power.

Be strong and of a good courage, fear not, nor be afraid of them: for the LORD thy God, he it is that doth go with thee; he will not fail thee, nor forsake thee.

Deuteronomy 31:6 (KJV)

We can rely on the power of God to turn things around. In hopeless situations, people take advantage of your situation to exploit you, financially and materially, even properties like house or land. People you relied on to solve your problem for you will pass at your back to arrange friends to buy your property using another name, even encourage you to sell it out and solve the problem. They want to buy your properties for cheap because they know you desperately needed help.

Some fake pastors too seize the situation to lie against the Holy Ghost that if you want your hopelessness to turn around, you must sow your landed prosperities to His church.

You will know them by their doings and fruits. Those who relied on other source of powers to solve their problems harvest much worse problems.

No hopeless situation can be worse than the situation of Lazarus, who died and was buried, yet Jesus Christ raised him back to life after three days in the grave.

Fake powers are harmful and discouraging people from believing the genuine power of God.

Fake men of God cause more depressions, more debts, and more sorrows to those who believed them.

❖ Rely on God's provision.

> But my God shall supply all your need according to his riches in glory by Christ Jesus. Philippians 4:19 (KJV)

In every hopeless situation Christians find themselves in, God is doing amazing things, preparing to send us help from Zion. He's our helper.

Abraham, in hopelessness; hoped in God's provision for a child. What about Hanna? Her situation was hopeless, and she was mocked by her people. Yet she resigned her faith to God and hoped on God's provision.

Any provision the devil gives you adds more sorrows. God's provision added no sorrow. The people you rely on during trials will always disappoint you, and you can never see them.

Our trust in man will yield no results. There was a man whose friend was in trial, and he needed a financial help. Long story cut short, he succeeded buying his friend's property at cheaper rate. You know who your friends are when you are in a serious problem.

In 2 Kings 4:1–7, the widow paid off her debts and lived comfortably well in time of famine. People wondered how come she suddenly became rich and paid her debts; God's provisions will take you from a mockery into a celebration. It takes you on equal level with those who mocked you and makes your life a wonder and a surprise to many.

> **And lest I should be exalted above measure by the abundance of the revelations, a thorn in the flesh was given to me; a messenger of Satan to buffer me, lest I be exalted above measure. (2 Corinthians 12:7)**

God was concerned about Paul not becoming proud. He, God, allowed thorns to happened to him to prevent Paul from becoming overexalted.

In verses 8–9, Paul reveals to us that in our 'thorns in the flesh' we should rely on God's provisions.

Satan never supplies you with anything to enjoy but adds bitterness and sorrow so enjoyment becomes difficult. Those whom he made rich overnight dies overnight.

Our God created everything and gave them to us to enjoy in peace.

❖ Rely on God's defense.

> "See, I am sending an angel ahead of you to guard you along the way and to bring you to the place I have prepared. Exodus 23:20 (NIV)

It's written:

> [9] He will keep the feet of his saints, and the wicked shall be silent in darkness; for by strength shall no man prevail. 1 Samuel 2: 9 (KJV)

What is your weakness in life? Maybe you don't have the qualifications to win battles or to be successful in life or you are afraid of your scary medical diagnosis.

Maybe your case was that of Paul's or David's. We all have weaknesses and shortcomings. When we find ourselves in weakness, we should rely on the power of Jesus Christ.

David heard about the giant Goliath. He knew that Goliath was a mighty man, full of power and strength, and well trained over the years, never lost a battle. David won the battle because he relied on God to defeat him. When we are weak, He is our strength. When we are afraid, He is our shield. When we are scared of diseases; He is our healer.

❖ Pray constantly.

> [18] And pray in the Spirit on all occasions with all kinds of prayers and requests. With this in mind, be alert and always keep on praying for all the Lord's people.

> Ephesians 6:18 (NIV)

> [3] 'Call to me and I will answer you and tell you great and unsearchable things you do not know.'
> **Jeremiah 33:3 (NIV)**

When things seem hopeless, pray until hope appears. The remedy to overcome a hopeless situation is running to God in prayer. Don't read love books or science journals when you are facing attacks from the devil. No matter how many love novels you read as a woman, you can never win the heart of womanized husband. But I assured you; If you can read the Bible and pray for your husband, that womanizing demons will hear your voice and flee. And as man, when you noticed that things are nose-diving, don't attend midnight meeting with occult men to solve your problem, but attend midnight prayers and do damage to all powers of darkness that are causing your failure in life

As God's prophet, am commanding your problems: that business failure, that bareness, that court case, that deadly sickness to stop immediately in Jesus name. As you say amen, It's done. Praise God.

Things may look like the brook has dried up. Men and women in the Bible went through hopeless situations and tough trials very similar to what we are facing today.

For example, God made provision for the prophet Elijah with food brought to him by ravens and water from a brook.

It happened after a while that the brook dried up, because there had been no rain in the land. (1 Kings 17:7)

Have you ever felt like your 'brook' dried up and God's provisions suddenly stopped? Are you struggling to make ends meet, or are you even thinking if God will still help you? All you need right now is to pray constantly until your prayer brings down the rain. Don't stop praying. Elijah prayed many times until the rain fell and the land wet back. God is ever ready to turn our hopeless to a pool of hopes. Don't debate your rising up with the devil during prayers. Apply the authority of Jesus Christ in you and reclaim hope.

❖ Make use of your 'handful'.

There is something called a handful morsel of bread of hope. When you find yourself in a hopeless situation, never fear to use what you have in hand, which may look nonsense. Grasp it, and use it. You never can tell if that morsel of bread is what God wants to use to give you hope.

A lot of people when they lose their better job remained jobless for years until the situation gets worse, and finally, they pack their things and return to the village.

If driving a cab is your morsel of bread, turn your private car into a cab; it will give you hope and put food on the table. There is no shame when you are trying to pick up the pieces of your life together. If you know how repair electronics, please tell people about it and get going with life.

There was a time in Europe, between 2017 and 2019, when there was a great economic meltdown in Italy. I was unable to get a job to feed my family, my wife decided to sell African food, like dried stockfish, and I started repairing old washing machines and sell them. Our ministry was greatly affected. Many members were out of job. It was hopeless, but God turned things around through a 'handful morsel'.

Sitting down and doing nothing about your hopeless situation is not faith but foolishness.

Everyone has a talent. During trials, use your talent to turn things around.

Losing your job does not mean you losing brain or your hand to do common jobs. Every great establishment owner started with small thing. It is unthinkable for any child of God to say, 'I am jobless'. God is not jobless. Drop your pride and start from scratch.

> **So she said, 'As the LORD your God lives; I do not have bread, only a handful of flour in a bin, and a little oil in a jar; and see:**
>
> **I am gathering a couple of sticks that I may go in and prepare it for myself and my son that we may we may eat it; and die'.**
>
> **(1 Kings 17:12)**

The Zarephath widow woman had almost nothing left, only a handful of flour and a little oil; the 'handful' was the key to her miracle.

Just as Elijah had to choose whether to obey God's instructions, so the widow he found faced a difficult decision when the prophet of God told her, 'Please bring me a morsel of bread in your hand'. (v. 11)

Hopelessness requires no debate with God's instructions and don't surrender to fear and unbelief but choose hope and obey God. If you want God to intervene in your hopeless situation and release his supernatural abundance upon you, be ready to make use of the 'handful'.

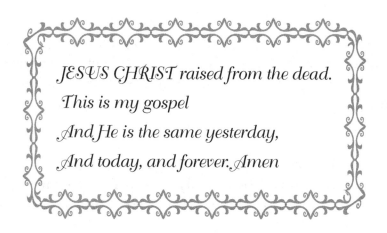

JESUS CHRIST raised from the dead.

This is my gospel

And He is the same yesterday,

And today, and forever. Amen

CHAPTER

The Power of Hope

What are you hoping to receive from God today? Everyone needs the power of hope to stabilise in this world of storms. Hope handled your frantic thoughts, and emotions make them harmless to your future. There is no problem that is bigger than hope.

If you know that you have a future ahead of you, place hope in front of you.

In our hopeless world today, we all need hope desperately. You can only obtain optimism when you make hope a subject of importance. Since in one's lifetime a hopeless situation is unavoidable, hope switches us into stability.

Our present moment may be difficult to bear, but it's better to bear it in hope on God's words than to bear it with sins—idleness.

> **For surely there is an end; and thine expectation shall not be cut off. (Proverbs 23:18**

Don't be afraid of the deadly circumstances, but you can only be afraid if you don't hope in God.

Hope builds our expectation high, and it does not fail. Three things are important: faith, hope, and love. Hope is the house that accommodates faith and love; hope is the parent of faith.

There is sadness, and there are good expectations from God. At the peaks of trials, you are expected to switch on hope because there's an end. Hope musters your faith to produce a miracle out of hopeless situation. Times of sadness and hopelessness require cherishing of desires with anticipation.

It means to desire with expectation of attainment. You know that good things are going to happen. Expect with a full confidence on the word of God.

> **Against all hope, Abraham in hope believed and so became the father of many nations, just as it had been said to him, 'So shall your offspring be'. (Romans 4:18)**

You must believe that nothing can stop it from happening. Good things must happen to you because your hope in God's words make them happened

> **'Return to the stronghold, you prisoners of *hope*. Even today I declare that I will**

restore double to you'. We are meant to be prisoners of hope meaning that we should never give up hope. (Zechariah 9:12)

Hope is 'powerful' because nothing is impossible with God.

❖ Hope is your future.

If you know that you have a future ahead of you to live, place hope and faith in your front. For without hope, there will be no meaningful future. Since your future is spiritual, and it is only God who knows your future, you must be a child God to have a God's-future kind of life.

Those who are not spiritual cannot understand where the future is leading them to. Hope, as spiritual force that causes us to keep moving on until our desires are met, encourages and inspires us to trust God and wait on His ways; He has prepared for us.

❖ God's hope makes you happy in a bad situation.

18Who against hope believed in hope, that he might become the father of many nations; according to that which was spoken, so shall thy seed be.

19And being not weak in faith, he considered not his own body now dead, when he was about an hundred years old, neither yet the deadness of Sarah's womb:

20He staggered not at the promise of God through unbelief; but was strong in faith, giving glory to God.

²¹And being fully persuaded that, what he had promised, he was able also to perform. (Romans 4:18–21)

You can't have hope in God and still look sad. True happiness comes from our hope in Jesus Christ. Abraham was very happy, and he never stopped giving God glory. Start praising God. You don't consider anymore what the situation is saying, but you consider the happiness the situation brings to your life. Think about Hanna in the Bible. She was without a child for years; she was the only woman whose son was called great prophet of God. She was happy. Nothing makes us happy than our hope in God.

Nothing makes us happy than our hope in God.

❖ Hope is strength of moving on.

Everything needs force or energy or strength to withstand the storm of life. Hope in God's word is Christians' strength. Since He keeps His promises and covenants and oaths, we must keep our hope, or faith or love to the end of our Christian race. We have no reason not to trust Him. Our God is dependable and trustworthy.

To survive the challenges of this world, hope must be our strongest weapon to keep us moving without tiring. There are times when the race seems tiresome, but if you have hope in God, His strength sees us through our dark times.

❖ Hope grows you spiritually.

Hope on God's promises grows our spiritual lives. Hearing the words of God reminds us of His faithfulness and ability to fulfil what He promised.

In absence of hope, your Christian life will not beam light. Show me a man of hope, and I will show you his spiritual level and promises of God he received.

❖ Hope heals.

The woman with blood issue refused to give up; even when the people she met or consulted gave up on her situation, against all hopelessness, she hoped to be healed one day.

> **²⁰And, behold, a woman, which was diseased with an issue of blood twelve years, came behind him, and touched the hem of his garment:**
>
> **²¹For she said within herself, If I may but touch his garment, I shall be whole.**
>
> **²²But Jesus turned him about, and when he saw her, he said, Daughter, be of good comfort; thy faith hath made thee whole. And the woman was made whole from that hour. (Matthew 9:20–22)**

She had spent all her money looking for cure but found no cure. Her situation worsened each time, but she refused to give up hope. She heard about Jesus Christ and said to herself, 'If I may but touch His garment, I shall be whole—healed'.

Listen to me, real child of God never sees any situation hopeless. If the situation looks worse or even dead or no life at all, your hope in His words will make the situation better again.

There was a man in the Bible called Lazarus, he was ill and eventually died. But when Jesus heard about his friend's dead news, Lazarus was confirmed dead by Jesus Himself. Yet, His hope on God to raise Lazarus from the grave is unshakeable.

> [14] Then Jesus said to them plainly, "Lazarus is dead. [15] And I am glad for your sakes that I was not there, that you may believe. Nevertheless let us go to him." John 11:14 (NKJV)

No situation is over unless you did not apply your faith and the power of His word to action.

Our Jesus Christ said: [4] When Jesus heard *that,* He said, "This sickness is not unto death, but for the glory of God, that the Son of God may be glorified through it." John 11: 4 (NJKV

This is the power of turning worse situation into glory – positive confession of God's words.

You determine what you want out of your issues. Our hope in God never shamed us but brought glory and honour to God.

As hopeless as the case of the man at the pool, he refused to return home not healed. He hoped that one day his turn to enter the pool would come, or someone would help him into the pool, and he would get his healing. This man hoped of healing so much because he saw people who came there, dipped themselves in the pool, and got healed.

> **[1]After this there was a feast of the Jews, and Jesus went up to Jerusalem. [2]Now there is in Jerusalem by the Sheep *Gate* a pool, which is called in Hebrew, Bethesda, having five porches.**
>
> **[3]In these lay a great multitude of sick people, blind, lame, paralyzed, waiting**

for the moving of the water. ⁴For an angel went down at a certain time into the pool and stirred up the water; then whoever stepped in first, after the stirring of the water, was made well of whatever disease he had. ⁵Now a certain man was there who had an infirmity thirty-eight years.

⁶When Jesus saw him lying there, and knew that he already had been *in that condition* a long time, He said to him, 'Do you want to be made well?'

⁷The sick man answered Him, 'Sir, I have no man to put me into the pool when the water is stirred up; but while I am coming, another steps down before me'.

⁸Jesus said to him, 'Rise, take up your bed and walk'.

⁹And immediately the man was made well, took up his bed, and walked. (John 5:1–8)

The worse your situation, the stronger your hope of recovery should be. Wait on hope all days, all months, and all years. The more you wait, the nearer is your healing.

❖ Hope builds our faith.

Behold, I am the LORD, the God of all flesh: is there anything too hard for me? (Jeremiah 32:27)

There is nothing our hope in God cannot achieve. Hope is a locomotive force that drives our faith high. If you want a bountiful harvest, plant your seeds with hope, for it is the soil you need to plant. Remember that not all soil are good for planting, but your hope in God says, 'Is there anything too hard for me?' You can plant anywhere you like.

> ¹⁰Lot looked around and saw that the whole plain of the Jordan toward Zoar was well watered, like the garden of the LORD, like the land of Egypt. (This was before the LORD destroyed Sodom and Gomorrah.) ¹¹So Lot chose for himself the whole plain of the Jordan and set out toward the east. The two men parted company: ¹²Abram lived in the land of Canaan, while Lot lived among the cities of the plain and pitched his tents near Sodom. ¹³Now the people of Sodom were wicked and were sinning greatly against the LORD.
>
> ¹⁴The LORD said to Abram after Lot had parted from him, 'Look around from where you are, to the north and south, to the east and west. ¹⁵All the land that you see I will give to you and your offspring forever. ¹⁶I will make your offspring like the dust of the earth, so that if anyone could count the dust, then your offspring could be counted. ¹⁷Go, walk through the length and breadth of the land, for I am giving it to you'.
>
> (Genesis 13:10–17, NIV)

In the above passage, it does not matter where or in what situation you find yourself in. What matters is your faith in God. Once you have put your faith in Him, hope for His promises.

Lot thought that by choosing the plain and watered land, he will do excitedly well than Abraham. What determines Christians' success is not what they study or what career they pursue, but their hope on what God can do through His promises.

> **Now to him who is able to do far more abundantly than all that we ask or think, according to the power at work within us. (Ephesians 3:20)**

> **But the LORD is faithful. He will establish you and guard you against the evil one. (2 Thessalonians 3:3)**

Nothing builds faith more than hope in Christ Jesus. Living a life without hope is building one's life without results. Faith can only be spiritually powerful if our hope in Him is spiritually powerful to guarantee us victory. Your faith can be shaken if your hope is spiritually weak. There are no alternative ways to make your faith productive than having hope as your solid foundation where God's promises are built upon.

> **Let us hold fast the confession of our hope without wavering, for He who promised is faithful. (Hebrews 10:23)**

HOW DO CHRISTIANS GET HOPE?

❖ **Make sure you are born again.**

Accept you are born again, and you receive faith from Him. You cannot not have hope on him. God is hope, and you can't have hope from Him without being born again. If you remove yourself from his branch, the source of hope, you will always see everything hopeless. I pray, as many that are born again, you shall overcome hopeless situations in Jesus's name.

❖ **Study the word of God regularly.**

> **For whatever things were written before were written for our learning, that we through the patience and comfort of the Scriptures might have hope. (Romans 15:4)**

Through reading the word of God, hope comes. Novel or magazines can never give you hope during hopeless situations. If you decide to drink as you like or smoke cocaine or join prostitution work because of your situation, you can never have hope but become more hopeless.

❖ **Believe God's promises.**

> **²I will make you a great nation;**
> **I will bless you**
> **And make your name great;**
> **And you shall be a blessing.**
>
> **³I will bless those who bless you,**
> **And I will curse him who curses you;**
> **And in you all the families of the earth**
> **shall be blessed.**
> **(Genesis 12:2–3)**

Abraham believed the promises of God, and as promised, he became the father of nations. He has already done it. As a Christian, if you don't have hope on the promises of God through His words, it means that you are not really His child. Every child has absolute trust on his or her father than any other person.

Whatever your father promised you, you will believe and be full of expectations. How much more your Heavenly Father's promises? God never lied, and He cannot lie to you.

Whatever He promised, He will do it. His promises are our hope. Remember that Abraham's case was even worse, humanly speaking, because he was very old, and his wife was old and past the childbearing age, yet the promise of God Almighty did not respect all that. She conceived and bore her husband a son according to the promise of God. Christians' lives are tied to God's promises. How can you achieve what God did not promise you through His word? If you achieved them without Him, it means that the devil gave them to you and be ready for sorrows. His promise to us surely comes to pass. Therefore, wait for His promises.

❖ **Be patient with God.**

Everything a man needs requires patience. If you are not patient, you may likely not achieve genuine and lasting results in this world. Since there is no one without trial, it means to get over your trials, you have to imitate those whose patience helped them conquer all tough situations.

> **[11]And we desire that each one of you show the same diligence to the full assurance of hope until the end, [12]that you do not become sluggish, but imitate those who**

through faith and patience inherit the promises. (Hebrews 6:11–12)

If you have patience with full hope on the promises of God's words, nothing is impossible to achieve.

Hope requires patience, and patience requires full faith and hope. Most problems of people were a result of lack of patience; they want to achieve everything earlier than God's time.

❖ **Don't stray away from the house of God.**

The house of God is the only place where you can get hope that will reassure you of better ending.

> **For I know the plans I have for you, declares the LORD, plans to prosper you and not to harm you, plans to give you hope and a future. (Jeremiah 29:11, NIV)**

> **And we know that all things work together for good to them that love God, to them who are the called according to his purpose. (Romans 8:28)**

I have seen those who called themselves Christians; they even speak in tongues, yet little temptation arose and they stop going to church. They sit at home every Sunday; they talk ill of men of God, argue blindly with people who visit them to speak about God to them. They find one excuse to justify their staying away from church. What kind of Christian are you?

Staying away from the church does not solve your problem; rather, you worsen it because no matter how you claim you are a self-made pastor, you can never solve your problem.

Some even stay away from the house of God for years, and they never bothered to repent and return to God. They see church as their greatest enemy and never find reason to blame themselves for their hopelessness in life.

If you don't want to remain on mockery lists of the enemies till eternity, run to the house of God and humble yourself completely before everyone, young or old.

Never you run from church of God for any reason. Demons and more problems will run to you. Once you run away from the church of God, you have ran away from Him. People who run from the house of God run into Satan's house—storms.

Their lives worsen as they live isolated lives.

It's written:

> [29] And God said, Behold, I have given you every herb bearing seed, which is upon the face of all the earth, and every tree, in the which is the fruit of a tree yielding seed; to you it shall be for meat.
>
> [30] And to every beast of the earth, and to every fowl of the air, and to every thing that creepeth upon the earth, wherein there is life, I have given every green herb for meat: and it was so.
>
> (Genesis 1: 29-30 KJV)

In the garden of Eden, Adam and Eve never sick or afflicted with pains or diseases The herbs that God created were given to man for food and even the animal or chickens are for meat. Nothing like using animal's blood for healing. The moment man committed sin against God , and He sent them out of His garden. Then, the devil whose plans was to see man throw out of God's protection and security, was waiting for man outside the garden of Eden with sickness, pains, sorrows and diseases. Man start to use the herbs in the field to cure himself. In the beginning there was no need to use herbs for healing because man has power over the devil – disease.

When you are in the house of God and you have faith and hope in Him, the devil fear to attack you because there's a divine protection upon you. But the moment you stop going to church because of minor offence, you will start to experience terrible pains and sickness. Don't ever run from God's no matter what. Stay at His presence.

If you stop going to church, it does not mean you can stop the problems and challenges in your life.

WHAT KEEPS OUR HOPE ALIVE

❖ Remember the past works God had done in your life.

This I recall to my mind, therefore I have hope.
(Lamentations 3:21)

We need to always remember the good things our God has done in our lives since we are born again. There are uncountable blessings our Lord God has done, and we need to remember these past victories; it will keep our hope alive in present challenges.

Bless the LORD O my soul and all that is within me bless His Holy name. Forget not His benefits. (Psalms 103:1)

You need to remember past victories in your own life and in the lives of others around us. When David was going to fight with Goliath, he remembered past victories. He said the same God who delivered him from the hand of the lion and bear will deliver him from the hand of the uncircumcised Philistine.

There is nobody under this earth that God has not done good for. All you need to do is to appreciate God for all His wondrous works and be reassured of His mercies.

You must not lose hope, no matter the situation of things. Never you allow the storm to dictate to you how to live your life. Never!

Once you keep your hope alive, you have kept your miracles alive.

❖ Refuse to accept defeats.

Our Lord Jesus Christ was never defeated. Neither did He allow trials to defeat Him. He defeated all powers—demons, principalities, and rulers of darkness—and made an open shame of them publicly.

Have the mentality of victory, no matter the handwriting of the devil on the wall.

> **And Jabez called on the God of Israel saying, 'Oh, that You would bless me indeed, and enlarge my territory, that Your hand would be with me, and that You would keep *me* from evil, that I may not cause pain!' So God granted him what he requested.**
> **(1 Chronicles 4:10)**

Jabez was born in sorrow, and he had difficulties in starting life. He started life in a tough environment, with no help from anyone. Everyone refused to help him. He was mocked, gossiped, and called a poor and worthless man.

He could have remained in that situation for years. Even he would have preferred to die. Many young pastors these days commit suicide because things are tough with them, but he chose to look unto God, and he prayed to the Lord.

> **Remember now, O LORD, I pray, how I have walked before You in truth and with a loyal heart, and have done *what is* good in Your sight." And Hezekiah wept bitterly. And the word of the LORD came to Isaiah, saying, "Go and tell Hezekiah, 'Thus says the LORD, the God of David your father: "I have heard your prayer, I have seen your tears; surely I will add to your days fifteen years. (Isaiah 38:2–5)**

Hezekiah was told by prophet of God that he was going to die, but he cried unto God and did not give up hope, and the Lord added fifteen more years to his life.

Then Hezekiah turned his face toward the wall and prayed to the Lord.

He believes God to a point that his faith in God's word reversed the irreversible. Hezekiah's faith and hope on God was an act of total war against a lost case.

The message of the prophet was not a joke but a sad news to a man of hope and faith in God. Prayer has corrosive acidic power to burn into ashes any unwanted particles.

Hope is a war against any hopelessness, no matter who delivers the message.

When you know your works in the house of God, you will remind God of your usefulness, and God will see the reason He needs to keep you alive. Any Christian who accepted defeats from the devil is not a material for pulling down strongholds. Stay on fighting until you defeat all that rise against you. Hopers live on hope therapy. They incubated themselves with faith.

❖ Read the God's words regularly.

The word of God is the strongest weapon that expressly delivered results without wear. It never gets tired, never gets old, never gets weak, and never disappoints those who trust the word. Once you decide to read the word of God, the devil is disappointed. Believe what you read and apply what you read because knowledge applied is power, then wait for amazing results.

If you read Shakespeare books when demons are harassing you, or you carry romance novels to read when your marriage is in a mess, do you know what you have just done? You switch on your room air conditioner for the devil to relax and sleep cool on your matter.

No matter how good the love song you sing for your husband, that will not make him not cheat on you. But praying against the womanising spirit in him will deliver him from harlotry and fornication's demons.

Stop reading romance books when you have late marriage problem or when you are constantly raped in your dreams by unknown person or spiritual powers. This powers can use your husband face or familiar faces to appeared in your dreams and make love to you. this is not a joke matter. The devil wants to destroy your marital life.

But the word of God you read regularly will send fire upon demons and evil powers.

To Him that believes, all things are possible to him that believes. (Mark 9:23)

Regardless of the situation around you, always keep the right perspective.

Remember what God said about the situation and rest your case.

❖ Magnify God through worship and praises.

Rejoicing in hope; patient in tribulation; continuing instant in prayer. (Romans 12:12)

Wherever there is joy, there will be hope. Praises and worship during troubled times will cause your enemies to lean and make them look unsettled. As a prophet of God who carries anointing fire of breaking curses, I curse the spirit of sorrow or sadness in your life in the name of Jesus.

I command every spirit of loneliness and depression to lose its grip over your life in the name of Jesus Christ. As you read my book, receive the anointing of God upon your life right now in Jesus's name. God will satisfy you with joy and unlimited peace. It's done in Jesus's name.

What the enemy wants from you is to deny the Lord God in the midst of your challenges and leave the fold of believers. Thousands of people have done that before. May you never face challenges that will take you out of Christ in Jesus's name.

❖ Fellowship with people who have hope in God.

You cannot fellowship with people who live hopeless lives and expect to live in hope. The people you move with have influence over your life. If you are moving with faithless people, you can never have faith.

Their lives will rub off on you, and gradually, you become like them.

If you want to make it to the top, spiritually select people you fellowship with and also your choice of partner for marriage or business. Your fellowship with the children of God, who are filled with the Holy Ghost, will surely keep your hope alive.

❖ Don't be ashamed to start all over again.

To be ashamed to pick up little jobs that is below your qualification is to choose

longsuffering for oneself. Start with what you have left in your hands. Never you wait for months to get befitting jobs. Hold on to the small job and move on. There is nothing wrong if you covert your private car into a cab; all that matter is that you have something that keeps you busy or doing something that puts food on the table.

Do you know that when men are jobless, their once sweet marriage start to develop cracks if unchecked? As a man, get yourself a job for the meantime. Otherwise, daily nagging and fighting cannot be avoided in the marriage.

To be ashamed to pick up less-paid jobs, when you lose your better job, is to be ready for your wife's insults and shameful character. Be ready to face the shame of not being able to provide for your family. Less-paid jobs, like driving cabs or cleaning works, can save you mental stress.

❖ Have a possibility mentality.

> **For as he thinks in his heart, so *is* he. 'Eat and drink!' he says to you, but his heart is not with you. (Proverbs 23:7)**

Let me say this to you who is reading this book: When you lose your job or you find yourself in a hopeless situation, get out of your home and go to a quite place for days and engage yourself in mental thinking and brainstorming.

Don't think about your hopeless situation, but think about possible ways to create jobs for yourself. Engage your mind and your brain seriously, and jot down flashes of ideas, and develop them as quickly as possible.

Every job you see around are handiworks of thinkers, not waiters. Waiters are employees, but thinkers are employers.

Thinkers change their situations; waiters worsen their situations. Your bad situation is subject to change once you decide to move on with faith and hope. There is no situation that someone has not experienced in life. It can't be only you who have experienced the situation since the world was created. Someone has been through what you are going through now and emerged victorious.

The fools will ask, 'If I keep my hope in God to fight my battles and nothing happens, what if my enemy repented?' I can't wait for God any longer. Something has to be done. Then you decide to involve criminal acts. Eventually, you find yourself in jail. Your hope is crushed by your foolish decisions or not taking action when necessary.

When you find yourself in a hopeless situation, think of the opportunity the situation comes with.

People lose their better jobs and they end up running their own businesses. Within a few years, they become employers.

You only lost your job; you did not lose your brain or your hands or your legs.

Thinks out of the box and get going. With your brain, you are not jobless, but you are on your way to create jobs for others.

Keep your hope alive by thinking out possible solutions than thanking people who feed you or give you pocket money.

As a pastor or child of God, you will be more effective in the kingdom works when you run your own establishment. Cultivate the fallow lands and keep hope alive.

In Jesus's name, I pray God restores all that you have lost.

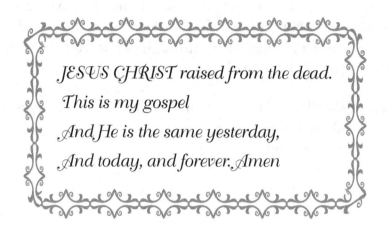

JESUS CHRIST raised from the dead.
This is my gospel
And He is the same yesterday,
And today, and forever. Amen

CHAPTER

3

Hope Changes Everything in Life

Everything you can see and the things your eyes cannot see are subject to change. There is nothing that cannot change, except change itself.

What changes our ugly situation is our hope in Him. What He says He will do, that's what He will do.

If nothing significant changes in your life after encountering Jesus Christ's power, it means that you are absent from His

House, the church, where He visits people to bless them. Or you are completely unreachable by the Holy Spirit.

There is no seemingly-hopeless situation in our lives that God cannot change, provided you have hope in His Son, Jesus Christ. Our hope in Christ Jesus has the power to change everything that is going on in the world.

A hopeless person has no hope in God or whose hope is on other gods.

Everything you have can be hopeless when everything you have are not from God. Hope responds to everything, hope produces chances of change, and hope does everything when it seems hopeless.

Christ's hope in us gives us the reason to live. It frames together our scattered dreams and visions. Hope strengthens our weak and fallible walls. Hope give us the power to lean on Him, and we become hopeful and great again. We are people of hope.

So make hope the handle of your door—life, then every good thing in life can easily be yours when hope opens the door.

Since there is a distance between you and your future, you need hope to join you to your future.

In between you and the storms of life, remember to wear hope as helmet of protection.

When you say that your situation is hopeless, you have slammed the door of restoration, and help from God may not come.

To walk on daily victory requires you to walk daily on His hope.

God changes everything for us when everything in us changes our hope and faith towards Him.

As a Christian, your hope in Him must mix with boldness, and remember that our boldness to change hopeless situations comes from understanding God's words.

Hear this: There is no shortage of Satan's powers—storms, sickness, disasters, failures, disappointments, and demonic attacks. Therefore, you must not have shortage of hope, faith, prayer, and trust in God. Shortage leads to failure in supply, low production, insufficiency, death, and finally shutdown. If a person has shortage of blood, he will fall sick until treatment is given. Once you have shortage of hope, you will likely fall sick—hopelessness.

Brethren, if you want to change unworkable things to workable in your life, apply hope as a force to change the course of things.

Everything will continue to move in one direction or at constant speed; if you don't like the direction where life has directed your destiny to, apply internal force of change—hope.

To not remain in one place or stay more than necessary on a spot, pray strange prayers that produce amazing results.

People actually stayed on problems for years. They go to church, do everything in the house of God, yet everything remains hopeless. You must pray prayers that are strange or dangerous. Such prayers are divinely designed to alter the interference of enemies in your life.

Our hope in God's words has the power to alter and to redirect our goals into God's purpose.

People who are around you may not want you to change your way of relating with them.

If you are affected by the way you relate with people, wait no longer and change your relationship.

Life can be so frustrating if you lack the power of hope to change things for your own happiness.

A lot of Christians never considered to wage war of hope and prayer against unknown forces that wrestle with them in life.

THINGS HOPE CHANGES IN OUR LIVES

> **But we all, with unveiled face, beholding as in a mirror the glory of the LORD, are being transformed into the same image from glory to glory, just as by the Spirit of the LORD.**
> **(2 Corinthians 3:18)**

❖ Hope changes our background.

I have heard people saying that their background is the reason why they are unable to obtain certain level in life. In every successful story told, there are unsuccessful beginnings. Your background is just like a photo studio background that does not show where you took the picture from. It is just a mere background. Everything on earth has a background, but it is not about what you are or where you came from or what your background say but what your new life represents or shows to people who once mocked you.

If you put all your hope in God, your poor background is irrelevant.

❖ Hope transforms us from trash into a better person.

Change cannot be hidden. When He gives us hope that makes things work for us, we are transformed from darkness into the light of our Lord Jesus Christ.

To live a better life is to first have a better hope in God. Great people in Christ are not hopeless, and we have this assurance that He transformed us into His own kingdom, and we are more glorious than what we used to be. Now there is a better joy, better promises, better start, and better end.

His hope in our lives makes us a better person, for He was the glory over Israel and still our glory forever.

❖ Hope changes our home.

A home without Christ is hurtful. People who are not children of God are children of daily abuse, and their homes are hurt with pain. A family that doesn't put their hope on God will not have the peace of God upon their home.

What changes our home is our hope in God and His presence. There is always overflowing joy in every home that hopes in God.

The troubles most homes are facing today is caused by parents and children making God irrelevant in the family, and not putting hope on God. Rather, they trust their wealth, and that is why you see the society rotting in crimes and violence.

The blessings of a changed home where Christ reigns is enormous. When looking for peace and happiness in our family, the family must be taught how to trust God completely and rely on Him alone. Then your home becomes a citadel of peace and progress. The key to unlocked your family potentials is to hope in God.

A disastrous home has no hope in Christ. Every crime in present society starts from the home, and the very day our homes turn back on God is when society is fueled with all kinds of atrocities.

The greatest problem of some people is hopelessness. Once you have poor hope that Jesus Christ cannot change your life, your reliance on your ability will make you commit crimes faster than necessary. To change our home from worst to the best, we must build everything about our home on God.

❖ Hope increases our boldness.

How do you intended to live life successfully in this world of bullying, hostility, and oppression? Do you know that we have more hopeless people in our society today? I mean, people are not interested to serve God or follow His will. People who have vowed to bring Christ's name down through evil laws. So tell me, how do you intend to live happily in the midst of vampire leaders that kill with satanic laws? As a child of God, you will face intimidations, limitations, and discouragements. To advance with the gospel, you need boldness.

Hopeless people are disengaged from possibility and disconnected from progressive ideology. If you don't want to be filtered from the world like dust from a vacuum cleaner, increase your hope in Jesus Christ. Hope is action spirit, and never submit to anything less than success. Boldness with hope in God sets ablaze every obstacle.

There is no man with hope who lacks boldness to confront critical situations.

Some people, after having their problems in life x-rayed, find it very difficult to find hope to change things around them. The situation will start to show resistant power, and then the problem will crush the person.

There is no situation, sickness or diseases or poverty, that is not afraid of your faith and hope in God.

You cannot achieve much from this world if you are not bold and a die-hard hoper.

To preach the gospel of Jesus to sinners requires boldness. To marry also requires boldness. You must be bold to make money. To do certain jobs requires boldness, and it takes boldness to face scandals and satanic petitions.

Everything man will ever need, or the level man wants to attain, requires boldness. There are scandalous and fault finders who are satanic in nature, and they are agents assigned to pull children of God down. In all your getting, get hope and be bold to win.

> **This is the confidence we have in approaching God: that if we ask anything according to his will, he hears us. And if we know that he hears us-whatever we ask-we know that we have what we asked of him. (1 John 5:14–15)**

If you have hope on something, you will build your confidence on it. Hope develops our confidence and boldness.

David defeated Goliath because he hoped in God; he was not worried about the bragging of Goliath but put his confidence on God. You cannot have a full confidence on a weapon that you do not trust or have not tested its capability.

We have hope in God because we have tested the power of His word and capability. No power can defeat Him. That is why our hope and faith remain unshakable even in the midst of trouble. We have confidence in Him at all times.

❖ Hope brightens our understanding.

Understanding the scripture is more powerful than a nuclear weapon. It is the secret of all believers' victorious lives. Hope is the light that brightens our understanding of things around us.

> **But Jesus beheld them, and said unto them, With men this is impossible, but with God all things are possible. (Matthew 19:26)**

Without you having the power of hope and faith through His name, you can never understand the powerful scripture above. Remember that Christ is our hope; therefore, His understanding becomes our understanding. Abraham had hope out of hopelessness because his hope power gives him the understanding of God's words and actions.

A perfect understanding of God's words makes our hope unshakable. In every bright future, there is an accurate and perfect understanding of the works of hope. There are works His hope does that no person understands but you.

Hope is our torch light that points us to His kingdom of operational systems.

You must understand a system perfectly before you put all your hope on the system.

Since Christians cannot do without knowledge and understanding, hope in His promises and words remains our only choice of understanding the functionality of the principles of this world.

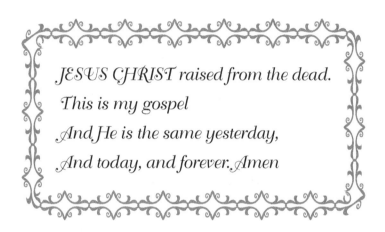

JESUS CHRIST raised from the dead.

This is my gospel

And He is the same yesterday,

And today, and forever. Amen

CHAPTER

4

Build Hope on The Little Start

Though your beginning was small, Yet your latter end would increase abundantly. (Job 8:7, NIV)

And though you started with little, you will end with much. (Job 8:7, NLT)

Your start may be insignificant, but you can end great if you don't get discouraged along the way.

Hope starts from little and grows into perfect dreams. You don't need to start big, with billions of dollars, but with Him with the little you have. You can build hope to a maximum level by relying on God's words.

> **But you shall remember the LORD your God, for it is He who is giving you power to make wealth, that He may confirm His covenant which He swore to your fathers, as it is this day. (Deuteronomy 8:18, KJV)**

> **The LORD makes poor and rich;**
> **He brings low, He also exalts. (1 Samuel 2:7, KJV)**

> **Furthermore, as for every man to whom God has given riches and wealth, He has also empowered him to eat from them and to receive his reward and rejoice in his labor; this is the gift of God. (Ecclesiastes 5:19, KJV)**

Hope can be developed through reading God's words, and you will not be afraid to start with the little in your hands, and God will cause His riches upon it. Little things that we neglected are our future empire if we hope on God's words. He makes poor and rich, so all we need is the Maker of wealth and prosperity.

Starting little does not mean you are small in thinking or your God is small or your ideas are small, but you recognise the fact that big things start from small ideas. Nothing big cannot become small, and nothing small cannot become big.

If watered with hope in God, every little start will end up big. Without hope in God, every big start will end up small and finally wind down.

Christians should not be afraid to start small because our God is a mighty maker of riches and wealth creator, who promised us bountiful harvests.

As a man of God, when you are afraid to start your church alone with your wife, a small congregation, you will remain a personal assistant of other men of God for decades. If you cannot manage a small congregation, you cannot manage huge crowds when God opens doors for you. And if you cannot hold little, you cannot hold empires. When you don't start with little, you wouldn't learn the secret of greatness.

You must be an experienced fisherman for you to catch big fish in the ocean.

Some inexperienced pastors are the cause of church breakups because they don't want to start with little members. When he or she breaks out of the church, half of the members follow them, and within a short time, the crowd disappears, and empty chairs are left behind because he or she lacks little principles to start.

HOW TO STOP OBSTACLES OF HOPE WHEN BUILDING WITH LITTLE

➢ Be persistent in prayer.

You cannot totally divorce your success in life from persistent obstacles. It's the obstacles you faced and conquered that pave ways for your mighty testimonies.

In every success–building, obstacles will build forces of pulling you down. If you are building something that will be worth of praises to God, opposition will surely attack you. You can only conquer them by putting your hope and faith in God as Nehemiah did.

> ➢ Don't allow extra baggage.

During building, unwanted expenses will come up just to distract you from focusing on what you are building. Time, family, and friends come up with their demands that you never budgeted for, but you must not abandon your plans because of excess baggage. It could be the devil who sent these demands just to stop you from continuing with your plan. Solution: Pray out all unwise spending from your plans.

> ➢ Fear no opposition—persistent fear of opposition.

Never you fear any foes when building a legacy. Nehemiah did not fear opposition when he was building the wall of Jerusalem.

When oppositions are saying you cannot complete what you started or they come strongly against you, deal with the opposition by praying constantly.

> **7But it came to pass, that when Sanballat, and Tobiah, and the Arabians, and the Ammonites, and the Ashdodites, heard that the walls of Jerusalem were made up, and that the breaches began to be stopped, then they were very wroth,**
>
> **8And conspired all of them together to come and to fight against Jerusalem, and to hinder it.**

[9]Nevertheless we made our prayer unto our God, and set a watch against them day and night, because of them.

(Nehemiah 4:7–9, KJV)

You must be an enemy to all your enemies by praying dangerous prayers at midnight. Command all opposition out of your way and cast them to hell fire. Don't fear them, but they should fear your God of war.

➤ Diffuse disappointments and frustrations.

If God is our Father who made heavens and earth, we need to learn from Him, His chief executive officer (CEO) in skills and strengths.

How He Started the Creation of the World from a Step-by-Step Approach

There are discouragements in everything in life: in business, church work, marriage, and career. You cannot totally avoid disappointments, no matter how good you are. The good news is that, if you put your hope in God, you can still achieve success or even rule in the midst of your enemies.

Build an altar of prayer before you start anything. Pray out discouragement, disappointments, and frustrations. If don't you take care of them, they will take care of your future, and you will end up with nothing.

Behold, I am doing a new thing; now it springs forth, do you not perceive it? I will make a way in the wilderness and rivers in the desert. (Isaiah 43:19, ESV)

God is ready to teach us His skills that make things work even with our little start.

He is ever ready to teach us how to do new things or greater things from our little start that people will praise Him for.

You don't need to have all requirements before you start; faith means starts, and hope for increase or blessings from God, the miracle worker. Those who wait until they have all the monies before they start will never start anything because the devil will not allow anyone, mostly Christians, to start. What you should do is have faith in God. When He sees your faith of starting with little, He makes a way. Don't despise the days of little beginnings.

I pray that as you decide to start with little in your hand, great increase will end it in Jesus's name.

➢ Remember that the power of God is available.

When you are starting small, remember that God's power is available to those who put their trust on Him; He will support you and protect your establishment.

When starting small or big, forces of struggle will act on you, but fear not. You have God's powers in you to conquer the forces.

Once God has spoken; twice have I heard this: that power belongs to God. (Psalms 62:11)

Don't look to the ground or around at what may fall on you or disappoint you when you want to get to the top in life. Remember: All power belongs to Him.

He brings the clouds to punish people, or to water his earth and show his love. (Job 37:13)

He loads the thick cloud with moisture; the clouds scatter His lightning. They turn around and around by His guidance to accomplish all that He commands them on the face of the habitable world. Whether for correction or for love, He causes it to happen.

Don't you think that God can fight for you with anything He chooses? He can bring calamity upon your enemies to punish them for touching you or anything that belongs to you.

Each time I see my life and what God has done for me, I fear God the more. I was attacked from both sides of life.

The devil entered my ministry through fake scandals to seal up my voice in the land of Italy so that nobody will hear my voice again. Those who the devil used came back begging me for forgiveness. The devil failed woefully.

The people I sacrificed my time to mentor and even helped with my own money were first to shatter the ministry. I was left alone to carry my cross.

I found strength and hope in His word, and I start the ministry again with three members, for I know that I can make it through His strength and grace, no matter what comes my way. God's power fought for me. I encourage young pastors who are facing membership challenge to look unto God, start with your family and pray against all evil powers frustrating your calling, then ask God to disappoint the devices of the wicked in your ministry in Jesus's name.

And you shall remember the LORD your God, for it is He who gives you power to get wealth, that He may establish His covenant which He swore to your fathers, as it is this day.

(Deuteronomy 8:18, NKJV)

I pray God will establish His covenant upon you again, and you will do greatly well.

HOW OUR HOPE IN GOD WINS

❖ GREAT THINGS START SMALL.

There are no great things until you start with small things, and great achievements actually start with our little earnings.

If hope mostly watered your little beginning, never you underestimate what your little savings can start to do. There is nothing wrong with starting with little at hand to get to the top, but everything is wrong if you don't start with what you have in your hand, no matter how little.

You don't need mighty or great efforts, but you need to start making an effort.

In every starting effort, there is always amazing harvest.

Achievers are not men of strength but are men of courage, and men of courage start with anything they have in hand.

Impossibility is not an issue in the mind of those who value small beginnings.

You can actually have a big mansion from the little foundation you laid. When you run away from little beginnings, ending big becomes a vision of night dreams.

Our Lord Jesus Christ started with few little fishes and seven of loaves of bread but ended up feeding four thousand people.

The big tree that you see today in the forest was once a seed planted in faith.

❖ AVOID STARTING BIG.

When you plan to start big at once without considering likely obstacles, you may not achieve your target or goal.

Remember that not all big starts actually end big. In starting big, you are likely to spread your resources and energy.

❖ ALIGN YOURSELF WITH CHAMPIONS.

Build one's hope on a little start that requires you to diligently search for champions who started with little and now have big establishments. You need their experiences and skills to guide yourself. Champions run to win, and they start celebrating at the beginning, not at the end. Goliath was celebrating his victory over David before the battle even started. When you have those who are Champions in fasting and prayer around you, success becomes easy. The reason why some pastors fall into temptations and could not rise up is because those who surrounded him are not prayer warrior but are just miracles or visions seekers. They did not come to build the ministry with the pastor but they came to solve their problems.

They don't accept good for best.

²⁴Do you not know that in a race all the runners run, but only one gets the prize? Run in such a way as to get the prize.

²⁵Everyone who competes in the games goes into strict training. They do it to get a crown that will not last, but we do it to get a crown that will last forever. ²⁶Therefore I do not run like someone running aimlessly; I do not fight like a boxer beating the air.

(1 Corinthians 9:24–26)

Champions are not pushovers; they don't associate with non-champions.

Align yourself with people who started little and are champions today. That is the only way for you to learn from them. You cannot gain anything from people who are not entrepreneurs; if you really want to add your name to the list of greats, look for a champion to learn from. If your mentor is not a champion in your field of interest, drop him or her. You will be discouraged because not all mentors are leaders.

As he was talking with them, behold, the champion, the Philistine from Gath named Goliath, was coming up from the army of the Philistines, and he spoke these same words; and David heard them. (1 Samuel 17:23)

Then David ran and stood over the Philistine and took his sword and drew it out of its sheath and killed him, and cut

off his head with it. When the Philistines saw that their champion was dead, they fled. (1 Samuel 17:51)

David was battle-ready to fight with a champion—Goliath.

Champions challenge champions; in life, whom you choose to get close with will either make you great or break you down.

David knew that an opportunity of record-breaking has come. He aligned himself with the greatest champion that no man has ever defeated and can never be defeated; He is Lord God Almighty.

David began his champion life by using hands to kill a lion. David refused to wear protective iron clothes or use a sword; rather, he chose insignificant materials, two stones and a catapult, and the word of God. The Bible says he ran towards Goliath with confidence and killed him with his sword. Mediocres never aim high in life; they settle for less.

❖ NOT BIGGER BUT GROWING.

The little beginning we started with may not appear significant or important, but don't look at the size of your little start. In years to come, you will be amazed with how it grows into a big establishment.

When you grow your hope on little start, the little beginning will grow big in a short time, and it will eventually keep your hope alive.

Everything you can see around that is big grew from a small dream.

Have the mindset of growing anything your hand finds to do; you never can tell that small things will keep you going in life.

God will always send rain upon our growing crops for us to be satisfied and give Him praises and thanks. Don't bother how it will grow into your dream desires, but be bothered how soon you can start. To be delighted in life is to light your ways through.

❖ NOT PERFECT BUT CHANGING LIVES.

> **But we all, with unveiled face, beholding as in a mirror the glory of the LORD, are being transformed into the same image from glory to glory, just as by the Spirit of the LORD.**
>
> **(2 Corinthians 3:18)**

The Lord changes us from glory to glory because none of us will ever be perfect until we get to heaven.

We must learn from God and grow with Him to achieve our desires in His kingdom. The little we started with may not be perfect, but our faith and hope on God's word can change our lives through it.

You may not have a perfect start; never mind, God will change things for you.

When you plant small seeds that you said may not do well because it's not good for the land, do you know that right on the ground, God is changing everything about the seed you planted? One day you will see a big harvest.

Never you worry about getting the perfect people, place, time, land, or faith. God is building perfect plans for you through your little start.

In our every little start, God brings out much fruits. In ministry work, pastors, though we are men of faith and hope, should not always expect crowds in our ministry after a year the church is established.

God determines church growth. He knows when to add crowds to His ministry.

Our duty is to preach the gospel of Jesus Christ in truth and faith. When you are in a hurry to have a mega church with overflow, you can't avoid dirty and sinful things. Many pastors have fell out of grace because their aim of preaching the gospel is fame and money, thereby making the church something like a business. Once a church has become a business, God is out of the picture. The purpose of the gospel is to win souls to the kingdom of God. When you are called and chosen by God, you will not be ashamed of starting little or be worried about the church growth as many do these days and fall into ritual practices.

God is the builder of His house, and we are employed to work in His house; the builder knows how to bring people to His house. Men of God who want to be exalted and are looking for fame, remember what happened to Paul. Thorns were given unto him to humble him. Pride is a killer of anointing power; and fame is the downfall of great men of God.

For every house is built by someone, but the builder of all things is God. (Hebrews 3:4, NASB)

86

Without God, your big ministry cannot survive the test of time. Even your little congregation can only become a mega church when you allow God, the builder of all things, to be your builder.

> **And he who was seated on the throne said, 'Behold, I am making all things new.' Also he said, 'Write this down, for these words are trustworthy and true'. (Revelation 21:5, ESV)**

If you don't want God to plan for you or teach your hand how to prosper, don't start with the little you have.

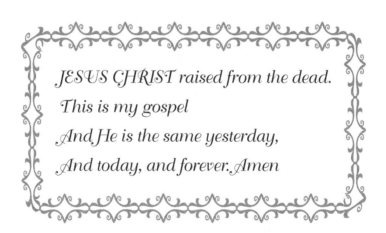

JESUS CHRIST raised from the dead.

This is my gospel

And He is the same yesterday,

And today, and forever. Amen

CHAPTER

The Prophecies of Hope in The Bible

❖ GOD GIVES US HOPE WHEN IT SEEMS HOPELESS.

God appears to Abram when everything about him was hopeless. Genesis 12 records the covenant God made with Abram. He told Abram to leave his father's homeland of Ur and follow him to a promised land—Canaan.

Abram and his wife Sara were childless and also poor. God said to Abraham he would be a father of a son. During this time, his wife Sara was very old and past the usual childbearing age. But God is not one to lie or will not fulfil His word.

His promises must come to pass. Abram was seventy-five years old, yet his age did not make him to doubt God. The promise about his son came to pass twenty-five years later, when Abraham's wife was ninety years old and Abraham was one hundred years old.

God's faithfulness is not bound by time or certain natural laws, but hope and faith bring promises to pass.

❖ GOD APPEARS TO US WHEN HIS PEOPLE DON'T KNOW.

What people don't know is that God's answers come when we don't expect it. God is faithful and full of mercy.

He sent His prophet to warn people of dire consequences of disobedience.

Some people were terrified with challenges, yet they don't listen to God or go to church anymore. So God sometimes allows enemies to conquer them and carry them into more captivity.

Some Christians complain bitterly that God has not given them miracles because they believe that God will answer them once their feet touch the church. God is looking for sincere hearts to bless, not miracle-seekers.

People who have no hope in God's word will always want to know when God will answer their prayers.

For I know the thoughts that I think toward you, says the LORD, thoughts of

peace and not of evil, to give you a future and a hope. (Jeremiah 29:11)

Moses, in Exodus, did not know that God would appear to him in the bush. Suddenly, God appeared and called Moses out of the burning bush. God never told Abraham in the dream that He is coming tomorrow to take him out of the land of Ur.

What about the lame man at the beautiful gate and that received his healing? God never told him that he would be healed by Peter on that day. Neither did peter and John were instructed by God or angel that they should go to the temple and heal a lame man.

As a child of God, we should not ask men of God or prophets the time or day or month to expect a miracle.

Do not be deceived by some pastor's boosting of anointing powers. Only God knows the time for our visitation, unless God reveals to His prophets, but remember, not on every occasion that pastors hear the voice of God or are instructed by God.

When you ask a pastor to tell you the time when God is going to answer you, it makes some men of God to lie to you and defraud you of your resources because the pastor knows that you are desperate of miracle.

It's written:
21 I have not sent these prophets, yet they ran:
I have not spoken to them, yet they prophesied.
(Jeremiah 23:21 KJV)

I encourage you to leave everything on the feet of Christ and continue to serve Him. If God cannot do it, *no* pastor or prophet can do it. So trust in God as Hanna did.

If it were possible to give children to a wife, Hanna's husband would have done that, but it's impossible with men. I pray in Jesus's name that God will appear to you and wipe away your tears.

❖ GOD APPEARS TO US WHEN IT COSTS HIM DEARLY

Our God is faithful and merciful. He sent His only Son to die for us and to save the world from sin. No matter what it may cost God, He is ready to restore all things for us.

In 1 Kings 17:7–9, God's words came to His prophet Elijah:

> **⁷Some time later the brook dried up because there had been no rain in the land. ⁸Then the word of the LORD came to him: ⁹"Go at once to Zarephath in the region of Sidon and stay there. I have directed a widow there to supply you with food".**

God knew the situation of the widow at Zarephath, yet He risked the life of his prophet to go there and ask for food from a woman who also needed food to survive the famine in the land.

Elijah, the prophet of God, knew that in Zarephath, there was hunger in the land, but he hoped in God's provision.

> **¹⁰So he went to Zarephath. When he came to the town gate, a widow was there gathering sticks. He called to her and**

asked, 'Would you bring me a little water in a jar so I may have a drink?' [11]As she was going to get it, he called, 'And bring me, please, a piece of bread'.

[12]'As surely as the LORD your God lives', she replied, 'I don't have any bread—only a handful of flour in a jar and a little olive oil in a jug. I am gathering a few sticks to take home and make a meal for myself and my son, that we may eat it— and die'.

[13]Elijah said to her, 'Don't be afraid. Go home and do as you have said. But first make a small loaf of bread for me from what you have and bring it to me, and then make something for yourself and your son. [14]For this is what the LORD, the God of Israel, says: "The jar of flour will not be used up and the jug of oil will not run dry until the day the LORD sends rain on the land."'

[15]She went away and did as Elijah had told her. So there was food every day for Elijah and for the woman and her family. [16]For the jar of flour was not used up and the jug of oil did not run dry, in keeping with the word of the LORD spoken by Elijah.

(1 Kings 17:10–16)

Once God has spoken His word, He must fulfil it, and nothing can stop it.

The prophet of God embarked on the journey, and according the prophecy of hope, Elijah and the widow were saved from the famine in the land until God sent down rain again.

The prophet's words turned the woman's life around; there was food to eat every day for the woman and her family and for Elijah. The jug of oil did not run dry according to the word of God. The prophecy came to pass.

If God can do it before, He can do it now. There is always a hope to be found, no matter how bleak or hopeless things may seem.

We may not know the time of God's visitation, but be strong in faith until He changes your situation for the better.

> **⁵And now the LORD says, Who formed Me from the womb *to be* His Servant, To bring Jacob back to Him, So that Israel is gathered to Him (For I shall be glorious in the eyes of the LORD, And My God shall be My strength), ⁶Indeed He says, 'It is too small a thing that You should be My Servant To raise up the tribes of Jacob, And to restore the preserved ones of Israel; I will also give You as a light to the Gentiles, That You should be My salvation to the ends of the earth.' (Isaiah 49:5–6)**

God sent His prophet to restore the preserved ones of Israel and to give us as light to the Gentiles. God never gets tired of paying the cost of our miracles, for He values us, and He is ready to do anything for us. God invested His Son Jesus Christ on us so we can preach the gospel of repentance and forgiveness of sins, for Jesus Christ is our salvation.

❖ GOD APPEARS TO US WHEN WE ARE ALONE.

The time of visitation is usually in the time of serious trials or challenges and sometimes when help may not easily be found.

> [22]That night Jacob got up and took his two wives, his two female servants and his eleven sons and crossed the ford of the Jabbok.
>
> [23]After he had sent them across the stream, he sent over all his possessions.
>
> [24]So Jacob was left alone, and a man wrestled with him till daybreak.
>
> [25]When the man saw that he could not overpower him, he touched the socket of Jacob's hip so that his hip was wrenched as he wrestled with the man.
>
> [26]Then the man said, 'Let me go, for it is daybreak'. But Jacob replied, 'I will not let you go unless you bless me'.
>
> [27]The man asked him, 'What is your name?' 'Jacob', he answered.
>
> [28]Then the man said, 'Your name will no longer be Jacob, but Israel, because you have struggled with God and with humans and have overcome'. (Genesis 32:22–28, NIV)

Jacob sent away his family and returned to his house to be alone and pray about his life. Then suddenly, a man appeared unto him and wrestled with him until his name was changed. You need a quite time with God when you are faced with disasters or destructive powers of enemies. Confront the problem with prophetic words of God, remind God of His promises, and hold on to faith.

Jacob's name was changed to Israel. You too can change that situation by you taking time out and be alone to pray and hear God's voice.

It's written:

> And call upon me in the day of trouble: I will deliver thee, and thou shalt glorify me. (Psalm 50 :15 KJV)

You are permitted to call unto Him in the day of your trouble. So, what are you still waiting for? Lift up voice and report the sickness or challenges to Him now. You will glorify Him.

Many Christians, instead of calling God, call more troubles into their matter.

They call in-laws, relatives, and friends who would not support God's decision.

Be alone with God and take the matter to Him in prayer; put the situation on the feet of Jesus Christ and consider it done.

God's appearance on our situation is the final whistle of victory. Once God appears to you, things will start to fall into place.

To be alone with God is to receive from Him the biggest and the best miracle.

Hanna was alone, and she asked for a male child, a prophet of God, and God gave her the best.

Listen to this: When you are alone, meditate on the word of God, never use your quite time to think about challenges, but read the word of God.

The negative thoughts of your mind are distractions and could kill your hope of receiving a miracle.

The devil often brings negative thoughts into the mind of those who face serious challenges. So when you go into quite moment with God, worship Him and praise Him for His mercy and grace. I can tell you that the devil is a stupid man, and he needs no respect from you. Kick him out of your life, please, if you want peace and happiness.

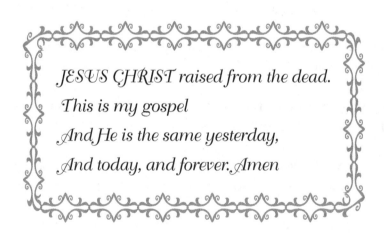

JESUS CHRIST raised from the dead.

This is my gospel

And He is the same yesterday,

And today, and forever. Amen

CHAPTER

What Hope has Done

There is nothing that hope cannot do. Everything about man's life is surrounded with challenges, storms, and struggles; the hopelessness of a man can be turned hopeful for meaningful and progressive life.

In life, there is nothing that God cannot do for the man He created. There is nothing too difficult for Him to do. But there are things God would not do in the life of a man for God's own reasons. We sometimes want things that God would not do for us, by all means, and that is why we often make mistakes in life.

Hope has done great and mighty things in people's lives, mostly in the life of Christians. The bedrock of life's greatness is hope in God's own time.

Our life attitudes make it difficult to appreciate God for giving us hope to live our life. In hope, our future springs out; there is no tomorrow for us if we don't have hope today.

The duration of people's sufferings is caused by lateness of hope in their lives.

As a man of God, I am opportune to meet with people with different problems, and I found out that before the trials or storms of these people get to the peak, hope was their greatest enemy. They were completely lost into the world of blaming life for every misfortune. Rather than looking for hope in Christ Jesus, they lost more into devilish things.

When you chose not to put your hope in God through His Son Jesus Christ, you have chosen to wallow with problems anywhere you go.

The legacy of hope is enormous in the life of a Christian. The only friend who will stand with you, no matter the storms, and ensure that your expectations are met is hope.

Hope is the bright light of our future in this world and the world to come. Hope has done so much for us: has taken away our sorrows and has made us fearless in the face of a deadly situation.

Let us take look at some legacies of hope in our lives:

❖ Hope gives future.

There is no doubt that this world is an enemy of the gospel of Jesus Christ, and everything in this world seems frustrating.

Whatever side you turn to, hopelessness is staring at your face.

What is future without hope in Christ Jesus? Everything that men are gathering or killing other souls to acquire can disappear in just a second.

Hope gives us future and still keeps it for us. There is no man with hope in God who is not successful.

It is only when you are sure of the future that you live it successfully. There is no man on the earth who knows the future, except God who created us. That is why Jesus said, 'for without Me you can do nothing' (John 15:5), meaning you are hopeless and futureless without putting your hope and faith in Him.

Our future is Christ Jesus, and our hope of entering the future is Jesus Christ.

Going into the future without hope in Christ is far riskier than coming into world at birth.

Future can only give you hope when hope gives you future. For example, if parents gave their children hope by training or sending them to school, the children will be the future happiness of the parents. Our future happiness is our hope in God.

❖ Hope is a shaping power.

The power to shape our hopeless lives is hope. The steering of our future is hope.

It drives us with its force into a bright future God created for us.

Hope shapes our shapeless situations and gives us glorious and a promising future in accordance to His purpose for us.

There is no promising tomorrow without you having hope today; future will not come unless hope first comes into existence to prepare the future for you.

Hope is a shaper, a restorer, and a repairer of things that seem hopeless.

When you discover that things are losing shape, and it seems you're losing it all because you don't know where to start from, start from hope to reshape your views and do the magic needed.

❖ Hope is a healer of future.

There is no serious problem on earth that hope in God cannot conquer. Hope heals our future when everything about the future seems hopeless and unachievable.

The man at the beautiful gate was lame and could not walk for forty years. He has resigned his fate to begging at the gate. So he never thought that one day his future will be glorious.

Peter and John believed the name Jesus Christ, and they have faith and put their hope in God's promises of healing the sick. Peter and John spoke to the man to rise and walk in the name of Jesus Christ; immediately, the lame man's ankles received strength.

When you have hope on something or power that you can never be disappointed, your faith will increase.

No matter how bleak the future may look, hope in God for better future. God has the power to command any situation to change, and His word will stand forever.

> **Who is he: who that speaks and it come to pass, when the LORD has not commanded it? (Lamentations 3:37)**

As sick as your future may be, the Healer (Christ, our hope) will give you more glorious future than before. Believed Him and give your life to Him; leave your future for Him to take care of.

I say this confidently: No man or powers—I mean, NO MAN OR POWERS OF HELL— can harm your future or deliver your future to disaster. Evil men or the devil himself may speak negative things but cannot stand unless God commanded it.

There is a moment in one's life that you will sit alone and be surrounded with bitterness of heart.

Never allow the bitterness of your heart to cloud your faith in Christ. Read your Bible and expel forces of fear or darkness from your mind; meditate on the word of God.

Loneliness, in the absence of God's word, often leads to complete hopelessness; and hopelessness amplifies your past faults, mistakes, and weakness and drains strength out of you.

Do you know that the devil himself is the most futureless and hopeless?

There is nobody the devil can hope on or rely on. He has no future to secure or work for. The only future hope the devil has is hell fire.

We, the children of God, have Jesus Christ, and we can trust Him for everything we need.

The devil has nobody to trust or hope on; on the last day, he will stand and face judgement alone. The devil knows that we have a glorious future, and nobody can undo it.

❖ Hope builds to last.

Hope of Christ was given unto us to build lasting faith in us till the Second Coming of our Lord Jesus Christ.

Do you know that our Lord Jesus Christ was the hope sent to this world to save all souls from destruction?

The Bible says Jesus Christ is 'the same yesterday, today, and forever', meaning, He was sent to last forever, from generation to generation.

God's hope, Jesus Christ, came as the last hope of man, and He came to build a kingdom of God that will 'last' from kingdom to kingdom, from generation to generation. Hope builds in us things that would last forever. Anything that will not last does not require us to put our hope on it.

When you wrote examination several times and you failed, and you are given one more chance to sit for the same examination, you will build all your hope on the last chance. The examination success determines your future forever.

Hope builds things that will last. The exam will define your future joy and happiness.

So your preparation will be greater than the previous ones.

You cannot build hope on a false foundation that will collapse overnight.

Imagine you laid faulty foundation. Your building will not be strong to withstand natural disasters like rain or earthquake.

Do you know that your future would not last or end well if the builder, hope, is not anchored on Jesus's name?

Anything that hope builds will last forever. Hope builds to last and not to perish.

You see people saying a project is their hope because they built it to last.

I encourage you to allow hope to build things that will last for you, but when it's not hope in God, it will not last.

❖ Hope is our defense against storms.

Our hope and faith in His word is stronger than any storms. Losers are hopeless, while winners, hopers, are giants of hope.

No matter how experienced you may be, storms of life will not give way.

Hope says all things are possible. Hope is the defense we need to braze up strength and to resist the devil.

If you are not defended in a battle with your personal hope in God, you will definitely not come back with victory.

Do you not know that life is a battle? Only those who have their hope in God win and come back celebrating.

No matter how powerful your weapons are during war, you must have hope in God.

Those who trust in horses or chariots never win battles of life; only those who remember the name of the Lord win every battle and also promoted.

It is not by human strength or knowledge that warriors are called warriors. They are called warriors because they know their weapons will never disappoint them. God is their weapon.

Hope in God and get His angels' patrol team over your life.

> **[3]He will not suffer thy foot to be moved: he that keepeth thee will not slumber.**
>
> **[4]Behold, he that keepeth Israel shall neither slumber nor sleep.**
>
> **[5]The LORD is thy keeper: the LORD is thy shade upon thy right hand.**
>
> **[6]The sun shall not smite thee by day, nor the moon by night.**
>
> **[7]The LORD shall preserve thee from all evil: he shall preserve thy soul.**
>
> **[8]The LORD shall preserve thy going out and thy coming in from this time forth, and even for evermore. (Psalms 121:3–8)**

We are safe at all times. No more worries, no more fears. God has commanded His angel to keep us safe, and nothing must harm us because we are the apple of His eyes.

❖ Hope saves nations.

When nations wander away from God's standard of living, and they take to infidelity against God, such nations never escape captivity.

Wickedness and sins forced nations into suffering for years. If the nations do not seek hope in God, they will eventually die by their enemy's or God's sword.

The nation that refuses to fear God will surely fall into disasters and will be taken captive by enemies.

If the nation returns to God for mercy and seeks God's face, there is restoration for such nation.

Jeremiah 29:11–12 assures us encouragement and hope:

> **'For I know the plans that I have for you', declares the LORD, 'plans for welfare and not for calamity to give you a future and a hope. Then you will call upon Me and come and pray to Me, and I will listen to you.'**

Jeremiah, the prophet of God, was faced with the destruction of the Jerusalem temple. He prophesied that God's covenant with His people would be a new covenant of the heart.

> **31'The days are coming', declares the LORD, 'when I will make a new covenant with the people of Israel and with the people**

of Judah. ³²It will not be like the covenant I made with their ancestors when I took them by the hand to lead them out of Egypt, because they broke my covenant, though I was a husband to them', declares the LORD. ³³'This is the covenant I will make with the people of Israel after that time', declares the LORD.

'I will put my law in their minds and write it on their hearts. I will be their God, and they will be my people'.

(Jeremiah 31:31–33)

Jeremiah prophesied restoration and new covenant, and the nation was saved.

Hope in God's prophetic messages brings restoration and peace upon the lands or nations.

If you will believe the prophecies in the word of God and repent all evil and return to God, there is restoration and peace.

The worst calamity usually hits the nations that deliberately refuse to repent evil ways and seek God's mercy. You cannot be praying for things to change and are still in relationship with the devil. Light and darkness have no relationship together.

To be saved from weeping and crying when it seems over, seek for God's mercy and repent all forms of wickedness.

Hope will only save you when you take hope as the only chance you are left with; weeping and crying are friends of hopelessness.

You cannot be an enemy of God's hope or anti-hope crusader and still expect restoration from God. The kings who accused the prophets of God because they prophesied hope and peace paid dearly.

If you want to be safe from disasters and storms of life, save hope in your life.

Those who see hope in Christ as a waste of time stay longer in their problems.

❖ Hope saves marriages and homes.

Abraham saved his marriage from disasters that would have made him lose God's own plan for him through hope in God's promise. Despite Sara's human solution, Abraham reminded himself of the importance of God's promises.

So Abraham kept hoping on the promise of His word, and his hopeless situation changed.

Have you ever experienced the bitterness and harshness of a woman looking for the fruit of the womb? It takes God's grace for any woman that is yet to have children to be accommodating. Some are always nagging and finding faults.

That was the situation of Abraham, and he did not know what do for Sara to believe God's promise.

If you don't have hope in God and if you don't humble yourself before man and God, your marriage situation will go out of hand. A woman who is always nagging and quarreling with her husband because he is yet to make her pregnant is wasting her time. She is simply telling her husband to go with another woman as Sara did to Abraham.

No man likes a nagging woman, and no woman likes a nagging husband. You are having malice and nagging in your marriage because both of you have abandoned God's hope.

Hope saved Hanna's marriage. She did not listen to mockeries. Neither did she fight her husband. But she had hope in a hopeless situation.

There is no amount of storms or challenges in your marriage that you cannot conquer with hope in God's promises.

His promises are true, searched, tested, and found fulfilled in the lives of those who wait for His promises.

Money cannot save your home from disasters. Beauty cannot stop your marriage from divorce. Gorgeous dresses can never stop a man from cheating on his woman. No amount of money in marriage can replace children or God's peace.

Money is not a solution to marriage crises.

Do you know that some rich men are very rude to their wives and insult their house helps? Such women are managing the marriage; likewise, men too. When your wife is richer than you, she does not fear God, there will be no peace in that home. She will turn her man into an errand boy or dishwasher husband.

I encourage every married man and woman reading this book to consider hope in God as the best wealth they need most. When you put God first, every other thing shall be added. Hope in God is the only saviour of your home.

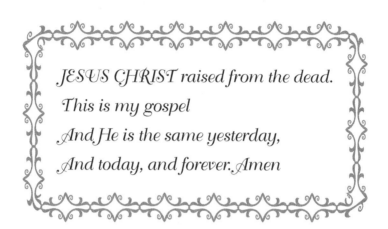

JESUS CHRIST raised from the dead.

This is my gospel

And He is the same yesterday,

And today, and forever. Amen

CHAPTER

Darkness In The World

**As dark as the world we live in, your hope
in the light of God keeps you shining.**

WHAT IS DARKNESS AND ITS ORIGIN

Darkness (spiritual meaning) simply means evil, total
disagreement with light, and destroyer of everything
light represents. Darkness is the opposite of light and its
representatives. Bitter endings are its rewards.

**Woe unto them that call evil good, and
good evil, that put darkness for light, and**

**light for darkness, that put bitter for sweet,
and sweet for bitter. (Isaiah 5:20)**

Anything that hates light, good things, and happiness in all entireties is what I call darkness. We must note also that darkness has forms and operates in different dimensions which we shall see later as we understand the whole meaning of darkness.

In the above verse, it is clear that darkness has nothing to do with good or sweet things, good environment, and cleanliness, but it's bad and evil. Whosoever lived in darkness can never see light as a friend and shouldn't be treated as one. The mission of darkness is to kill the truth, steal evidence of justice, completely destroy sweetness out of the earth through evil agents.

THE FIRST DARKNESS

**In the beginning God created the heavens
and the earth. Now the earth was formless
and empty, darkness was over the surface
of the deep, and the Spirit of God was
hovering over the waters. (Genesis 1:1–2)**

In the beginning, the whole place was empty, and there was total darkness.

The darkness was formless, empty, and harmless but with energy that gives the dark a power to be over the deep. The energy was denser than any known fluids. It was mighty and in the form of packets of waves. These waves come from all directions at a high, constant, and absolute speed. Nothing actually existed yet apart from the waters. The only existing force was the spirit of God.

The earth had no form at all; the waters were flowing in all directions.

Waters existed, but like the earth, they were also as yet unformed. The only visible thing then was the waters. All was dark. The first evening, darkness throughout nature, is called night. The description of the physical situation in the first verses of creation narrative is correct in every detail. What was called *night* and *evening* is simply darkness, prevailing throughout the universe for an unspecified period.

Small minds may say or dismiss the insight meaning of creation as trivial, but great minds will note carefully that the earth existed in a formless emptiness and was dark, but the darkness was not as wicked and bad as we can see today. If we say darkness is merely the absence of light, then darkness is nothing. Remember that the absence of anything needs no creation. One may take the first line of Genesis, *In the beginning, God created the heavens and the earth,* and verse 3, *And God said, 'Let there be light, and there was light',* as a summary of the creation narrative.

When you read verse 2, *And the earth was without form and void, and darkness was upon the face of the deep. And the spirit of God moved upon the face of the waters,* it describes the condition of the earth before there was light. The earth was formless, empty, and dark, but it was not mere nothingness. It makes much more sense to consider the first verse as the narrative of an act of divine creation at the very beginning and the appearance of light at a later time as the first visible result of formation.

ORIGIN OF DARKNESS

Why darkness comes first? Darkness came first to mark the beginning of a day.

This was the thought of Moses, the writer of Genesis, and it took him a stroke of genius to understand that the earth existed in darkness before there was light.

The greatness of Moses's ideas about creation helped man understand that darkness or dark was not evil. Three Bible scholars studied the creation narrative and gave their own interpretation. Each one added a valuable insight to the creation story.

They were the prophet Isaiah; Saul of Tarsus, who became the apostle Paul, and the apostle John.

The creation of darkness, according to Isaiah (45:7), 'God says, I form the light, and create darkness: I make peace, and I create evil: I the Lord do all these things'.

> Here, God says through Isaiah that He creates *darkness*. God created everything that exists. No one created Him. But according to Moses, just after the beginning, darkness is an existing substantive part of the heavens and the earth.
>
> **⁵This is the message we have heard from Him and announce to you, that God is Light, and in Him there is no *darkness* at all.**
>
> **⁶If we say that we have fellowship with Him and yet *walk in the darkness*, we lie and do not practice the truth; ⁷but if we walk**

in the Light as He Himself is in the Light,
we have fellowship with one another, and
the blood of Jesus His Son cleanses us from
all sin. (1 John 1:5–7, NASB)

⁵This then is the message which we have
heard of him, and declares unto you, that
God is light, and in him is no darkness
at all.

⁶If we say that we have fellowship with
him, and walk in darkness, we lie, and do
not the truth.

⁷But if we walk in the light, as he is in the
light, we have fellowship one another, and
the blood of Jesus Christ his son cleanseth
us from all sin. (1 John 1:5–7, KJV)

In the above report of Apostle John, darkness is a symbol of
sin and evil. In God, there is no darkness (sin), and you must
not allow darkness—sin—to be in you because there is no
darkness in our God. If we don't take our freedom back from
the devil by decamping from kingdom of darkness to light,
and walk in righteousness through His Son Jesus Christ, our
fellowship with God will always be unstable.

DARK BUT NOT EVIL

In many places in the Bible, darkness is a symbol of evil. But
if we read Isaiah 45:7, God says that He creates evil. But the
darkness Moses talks about in the beginning was not evil but
a substantive part of the heavens and the earth. In Moses's

narrative of creation, God frequently pauses to evaluate what He has made, and everything He has made is always *good*.

God saw all that He had God made, and it was very good. (Genesis 1:31)

Everything God made, including darkness, was very good. Therefore, the darkness God created was also good. Some people spiritualise the darkness of Isaiah 45:7 and take it as evil, but that leads to logical difficulties. Isaiah 45:7 is physical and literal. Isaiah is talking about the kind of darkness and light that a child with seeing eyes understands.

God saw that the light was good, and he separated the light from the darkness. (Genesis 1:4)

The light did not eliminate the darkness or remove it completely from the earth's architectural designs of the world, and because it was good, not evil, God kept the darkness and the light, but He separated them. Separation can be done in time or in space or both. The darkness and the light were good. We will see later other kinds of darkness and see why they are evil.

FORMLESS, EMPTY, AND DARK

Isaiah doubtlessly meditated on Genesis 1:1–3 when he wrote that God creates darkness and forms light. In the beginning, when the heavens and earth were created, they were, at first, formless, empty, and dark, but they existed.

The Bible says that the earth was *formless, empty,* and *dark*. The unformed earth, at first, existed in an empty and dark space but not evil. Moses did not tell us that the darkness that was upon the waters was evil, and if it was evil, God's spirit would have guided the earth and the heavens from the evil darkness.

HOW DID THE DARK, IN THE BEGINNING, BECOME EVIL?

The dark world that God created was without evil. It was without any form of wickedness or harmless to other creations, like the waters, the light, and the heavens. These were the only existing creations, as at that time, man, fish, or birds were created yet.

The creation of man brought sin into the peaceful world; man's mind and his desires let down sins, and sin caused man to walk on the path of wickedness.

Whatever that feared man in the beginning became man's fear. In the garden of Eden no animal or reptile was dangerous to man but were loyal, obedient and friendly to man. But the moment man commit a sin, the animals and reptiles were no longer loyal to man. Snake or Scorpion becomes man's enemy. Our exposure to sin is deadly as a virus.

Darkness (devil) only helped man achieve his sinful desires. The mental thinking of man is about accomplishing the desires of his mind, so the mind of man became prospered with evil and wickedness.

Man is the creator of darkness—evil, sickness, poverty, and hatred. The development of evil skills in darkness laboratories—covens, evil altars, and demonic temples (occults), where man acquired powers—further engineered man to do more wickedly to himself and his neighbors.

The world was only in a dark state until man made its darkness through sins and evil.

KINDS OF DARKNESS

Darkness as a symbol of sin

Darkness is often used in scripture as a symbol of sin. It is often contrasted with light, symbol of forgiveness and the presence of God.

> **[19]And this is the condemnation, that light is come into the world, and men loved darkness rather than light, because their deeds were evil. [20]For everyone that doeth evil hateth the light, neither cometh to the light, least his deeds should be reproved (exposed). (John 3:19–20)**

For every dark deed a man loves, he is risking it all in life. There is no good ending evil deeds have ever produced. Sin is complete darkness. The most sad thing is that everyone born into the family where dark things are done never considered light or accepting Christ to be important.

No evil deeds shall go unpunished, and life is always hard on them and their children unless the children turn to light— Christ Jesus. Parents who harmed other people's children with dark powers never see their children's success. Check out their children. They never succeed in life, no matter the educational levels obtained. The evil of their parents stop them from progressing and eventually die the same way their parents died.

In any way you look at it, the most wicked and dangerous evil charms are cast on people at night. That is why Christians must pray against midnight powers for a victorious life.

> **¹²To deliver you from the way of evil. From the man who speaks perverse things.**
>
> **¹³From those who leave the path of uprightness. To walk in the ways of darkness.**
>
> **¹⁴Who rejoice in doing evil. And delight in the perversity of the wicked;**
>
> **¹⁵whose ways are crooked. And who are devious in their path. (Proverbs 2:12–15)**

You are not completely safe from dark embarrassment unless you genuinely repent all forms of wickedness. But this physical world where wickedness is staring at you from all directions living a completely dark free life becomes a mirage. That is why the light came on its own to deliver us from the way of evil—darkness and men who surrounded us or live in our environment who speak or command evils to attack the innocents. Note: Not everyone in your compound are light, and the more dark people in your area, the riskier your infection rate with evil things is. This is why society often has evil men at the top of leadership.

Those who walk in crooked ways enjoy wickedness and do evil to the few innocents.

Child of God, fear no more. There will be joys and hope. The light came to shine around you and to deliver you from all works of darkness. See also Proverbs 4:19 and Isaiah 5:20.

Darkness as a symbol of ignorance of the truth

In whom the god of this world hath blinded the minds of them which believe not, lest the light of the glorious gospel of Christ, who is the image of God, should shine unto them. (2 Corinthians 4:4)

The devil is the god of this world system that is ruling, causing confusion, and creating disasters and pains.

The inhabitants of the earth gave their lives to darkness ignorantly because Satan promised them wealth, powers, and protection; all these are what man seek after.

The word of God says, 'But seek for the kingdom of God and His righteousness, and all these things shall be added to you'. (Mathew 6: 33)

Only fools seek after what was rightly given unto them. You cannot ask for what is in your hands. The day you gave your life to Jesus Christ, and you forsake all wickedness, and you stay on righteousness path, you are powerful than trillions of demons or powers. Darkness never consumed light, but light did. The eyes of all evildoers are blind to the truth and reality of the Son of God, the light. Their minds never see anything wrong in what they do. Only the light sees and understands all things wickedness does.

⁴Deliver the poor and needy; rid them out of the hand of the wicked.

⁵They know not, neither will they understand; they walk on in darkness: all

the foundations of the earth are out of course. (Psalms 82:4–5)

It is sad seeing some Christians, after many years in the church, still lacking understanding and asking questions like uneducated Christians when they are supposed to be graduates of Holy Spirit's university, faculty of all knowledge, understanding, and wisdom.

God delivered us from out of the hands of the wicked and evil men. Our keeper never sleeps nor slumbers.

Understanding is the cure of ignorance and false teachings. Satan never near-deceives those who know the word of God.

This is the end of the matters. Satan has no understanding of the truth, and anyone who chooses his ministry—ignorance— will always live in sin and do only wickedness. See also Isaiah 8:20, 2 Corinthians 3:14–15, and Ephesians 4:18.

Darkness as a symbol of the inability to find the right way

> **Then Jesus said unto them, Yet a little while is the light with you. walk while ye have the light, lest darkness come upon you for he that walketh in darkness knoweth not wither he goeth. (John 12:35)**

Christians are the light of this world, and we are created to show the wicked the way of the Lord. The ability to find a way out of critical situations, the light of God, is in us. Where there is light, no darkness is permitted to walk, not even around it.

The supernatural light, with all powers, shines on the believer's ways.

Anybody who refuses to carry a lamp or torch light on a night journey will miss the way to their destination.

You need to examine the journey you are in now: marriage, business, church you attend, anything you plan to do. Find out first if you are not walking in darkness or you are not walking with dark people because the journey will lead to nowhere.

If you have the light of God in you, be cautious of people who walk with you, for they may likely take you back to darkness. Unserious Christians in the house of God will fall into a dark path where darkness will fall upon them. Every right path in life requires the right light to walk on the path fearlessly 'til the end.

You are the light of the world. A city that is on the hill cannot be hidden. (Matthew 5:14)

In darkness, sin, and evil, good things are hidden from being seen, like you can never see the beauty of a woman in the darkness. Truth and facts are hidden in darkness, but in light, truth is seen and facts are opened. Beauty never hides in the presence of light. We are the beauty of the world. Light says it all about you. Read also Job 12:24–25 and Isaiah 59:9–10.

Darkness as a symbol of times of trial

In any darkness you are going through, there is interference of afflictions, spells, curses or trials and manipulations from the temples of evil or darkness powers. Darkness is the symbol of trials. Ask any man who is in trial how he get into the mess, and he will tell it's the devil or sin.

> **Such as sit in darkness and in the shadow of death, being bound in affliction and iron. (Psalms 107:10)**

Darkness is a complete bondage, and only the light of the Son of God can set you free. Afflictions and trials are often the early symptoms of darkness in operation, and if not checked, it comes with death. There is no affliction or trial that does not bring people down from the top to the ground. Walking with people of evil powers of darkness is a suicide mission. The valley of the shadow of death is the grave that swallows those who are in darkness.

The word of God says, 'Yea, though I walk through the valley of shallow of death, I will fear no evil: for thou art with me, thy rod and thy staff they shall comfort me'. (Psalms 23:4)

You can't conquer all afflictions and trials if you deviate from the path of light.

> **But if any live many years, and rejoice in them all, yet let him remember the days of darkness, for they shall be many. All that cometh is vanity. (Ecclesiastes 11:8)**

In the college of trials and afflictions, only those who have light and walk in the light graduate with testimonies. Actually, trials of believers command outstanding testimonies. Those whose walks and their ways are filtered with sins can never escape the day of darkness—afflictions and death.

Darkness as a symbol of death and the grave

> **20Are not my days few? Cease then, and let me alone, that I may take comfort a little.**

122

²¹**Before I go where I shall not return, even to the land of darkness and the shadow of death;**

²²**A land of darkness, as darkness itself, and of the shadow of death, without any order, and where the light is as darkness.**

(Job 10:20–22)

In the land of darkness, evil, wickedness, and death surround it. The prisoners of darkness never get paroled by Satan. But God frees and delivers all prisoners out of the bondage of darkness.

The belief of wicked people is that their dark powers can save them from punishment, that the wealth they laboured to get in evil ways will last.

¹⁰**For he seeth that wise men die, likewise the fool and the brutish person perish, And leave their wealth to others.**

¹¹**Their inward thought is, that their houses shall continue forever, and their dwelling places to all generations; they call their lands after their own names. (Psalms 49:10–11)**

Evil people are surrounded with painful death, and the end of all evils or darkness plot against the innocent is failure. It's written, 'No weapon formed against me shall prosper'.

So you need not be bothered about satanic plots; hope in God's words.

Every encouragement you received from Satan is to lure you into its trap where he can have full access to your soul.

Brethren, fear not the works of darkness, but the works grace has done for you.

See also Psalms 88:10–12 and Psalms 49:19

GOD'S PROVISION FOR HIS CHILDREN DURING TIMES OF DARKNESS

God himself is a remedy for darkness.

> **For thou art my lamp; O LORD: and the LORD will lighten my darkness. (2 Samuel 22:29)**

> **Rejoice not against me, o mine enemy when I fall, I shall arise; when I sit in darkness; the LORD shall be a light unto me. (Micah 7:8)**

> **28For thou wilt light my candle: the LORD my God will enlighten my darkness.**

> **29For by thee 1 have run through a troop; and by my God, have I leaped over a wall. (Psalms 18:28–29)**

See also Psalms 30:5.

Everyone who puts their trust in God wins all afflictions and trials.

What Christians carry, the Holy Spirit, is too powerful for the devil or the so-called affliction to handle.

God is our immediate remedy to all dark powers. Satan knew that once our light is switched on, darkness bows, irrespective of the nature of the disease, affliction, or trials.

We are guaranteed by His words, a total dominion over powers of darkness. The only requirement is to enroll in the college of faith for a total victorious life and you must accept Jesus as your Lord and Saviour early in your life.

You can leap over walls of difficulties, you can actually defeat wicked troops like demons and witches, and you will be untouchable forever.

You have the light of Christ in you to shine in the midst of tough situations.

God delivered us from darkness.

> **The people that walked in darkness have seen a great light: they that dwell in the land of the shadow of death, upon them hath the light shined. (Isaiah 9:2)**

> **[17]Delivering thee from the people, and from the Gentiles, unto whom now I send thee,**

> **[18]To open their eyes, and to turn them from darkness to light, and from the power of Satan unto God, that they may receive forgiveness of sins, and inheritance among them which are sanctified by faith that is in me. (Acts 26:17–18)**

> **Who hath delivered us from the power of darkness, and hath translated us into the kingdom of his dear Son. (Colossians 1:13)**

It is a spiritual error for a changed man in spirit, mind, and knowledge to remain unchanged or nontranslated. The moment the Son of God changed us into His kingdom, royal laws are signed and sealed.

We become legal residents in the kingdom of God. Then He called us His own.

Your changed life now has dominion right and powers over darkness.

Let me tell you something here: Every child of God who wears the royal dressings of God's kingdom can never wear the apparels of darkness again. The idiot witches do confess that they wear witch clothes on people to torment them. Can you wear evil clothes on burning flames of fire? Even iron-made clothes will be burnt into ashes in the fire. Do know that the Holy Ghost's fire is in your body? It is difficult for the most powerful witch to wear witch clothes on an ordained man of God. We are incubated with unlimited power that Satan cannot be near to or withstand.

We have been ordained as princes and princesses in God's kingdom, and this spiritual status makes darkness tremble and bow.

Hear this now: The power of any kingdom or evil altars depends on the power made available to the kingdom. Once the man who heads the kingdom is powerless, the kingdom is also powerless.

The available powers of any kingdom determines the longevity or duration of that kingdom. The kingdom of God has unlimited powers and authorities, from generation to generation, and His powers are without end. Therefore, Christians have unlimited power to undo what any dark power has done. See also 1 Thessalonians 5:4–5.

God's Son saves believers from darkness.

Then spake Jesus again unto them, saying, I am the light of the world: he that followeth me shall not walk in darkness but shall have the light of life. (John 8:12)

For ye were sometimes darkness, but now are ye light in the LORD: walk as children of light. (Ephesians 5:8)

Everyone who does not accept Jesus Christ as Lord and personal Saviour is completely living in darkness and has no light in Him.

Darkness will always hurt those who reject the gospel of Jesus Christ.

The worst and unacceptable embarrassment that Christians must not take from Satan is intimidation of his powers.

By His blood, our Lord Jesus Christ saves us from all darkness, harassment, and torment.

You cannot intimidate a man with destructive spiritual weapons that are invisible to carnal minds to attack. It's only a fool who will attack a man with dangerous and undefeated weapon. Once you have been delivered from something, you are superior to that thing, and its fear no longer scared you, but your fear is feared. See also

John 1:4–5 and John 12:46.

God's people rescue others from darkness.

> **⁶I the LORD have called thee righteousness, and will hold thine hand, and will keep thee, and give thee for a covenant of the people, for a light of the Gentiles.**
>
> **⁷To open the blind eyes, to bring out the prisoners from the prison, and them that are sit in darkness out of the prison house. (Isaiah 42:6–7)**

God called you and me righteousness. Praise God. Nothing can ever call me unrighteousness. My hand is in His hand, and He takes me to high places in life.

I can't live a low-profile life. It's impossible. I am light, a symbol of His glory. I am a rescuer. I am an undefeated man of God.

I carried the power of grace to get other people from darkness and to open prison houses and to set prisoners free. I am trained by Jesus Christ to save others.

All Christians are rescue teams of God to free people from darkness and prison houses like witch covens and satanic altars and shrines. Hallelujah!

> **¹Arise and shine; for thy light is come, and the glory of the LORD is risen upon thee.**
>
> **²For, behold the darkness shall cover the earth, and gross darkness the people but the LORD shall arise upon thee, and his glory shall be seen upon thee. (Isaiah 60:1–2)**

Fear not what covers the earth, but always remember that the gospel of Jesus came to dominate the earth and to wipe out darkness forever.

So declare this: No matter what happens to the earth, I and my family are excluded. We are wonderfully and fearfully created. It is not negotiable and undeniable.

The glory of God must be seen in you.

Our rising is not determined by the level of wickedness or evil surge we undergo.

The spoken word of God has commanded our victories even before we are born.

The word of God has the capacity to perform all He said in the capability of the Holy Spirit. Listen to this: Every light, be it sunlight, candlelight, car light, or village lamp light, has the power to chase away darkness. When light appears, darkness becomes irrelevant. Do you know that the more of His light in you, the more evil powers become irrelevant, the more they lose capability to harm.

THE OPERATIONAL MECHANISM OF DARKNESS AROUND US

> ➤ Darkness operates as sickness or diseases in people's bodies

This type of darkness defies all medical solutions and sometimes resists spiritual solutions—prayers. But with God, all things are possible. In a situation like this, children of God must come together to fast and pray aggressively, not leaving the battle for the pastor only.

➢ Darkness operates as a constant failure

Darkness can be failure in homes, churches, and nations or land. Failure is the end product of darkness. When you are experiencing constant failures in the midst of much opportunities despite labour or energy to achieve success, yet failure keeps ravaging your works, rise and draw the battle line against all midnight powers.

➢ Darkness operates as disappointments

There are a times when one may experience disappointments either for the will of God to stand or our inability to have all requirements to succeed. But when you are disappointed in every area or all areas of life, like being unable to stay in a marriage, or each time you get a job, you get fired within a short period or sacked some reason, or you are always squatting with friends every few years, or you are above marrying age, something is wrong.

In everything you do, disappointments end your efforts; the powers of darkness are operating in your life or around you. Christianity is about fasting and prayer, not about speaking in tongues alone. You can speak in millions of tongues and still remain childless, homeless, and jobless. These setbacks are the operational systems of the enemies to stop your star from shining.

➢ Darkness operates as hatred

People experienced hatred without course or reasons. Do you know that people under the influence of the manipulation of darkness hate themselves? They never see anything good about themselves. Such people always commit suicide. As a man of God, I have seen cases of people with the spirit of hatred;

this spirit was cast upon them by the power of darkness, and nothing good they say that will not annoy people.

➢ Darkness operates as curse

Curse is not a blessing but an evil thing. Once it's placed on someone, the power of darkness starts to operate in the destiny of the person. A curse is worse than darkness. It goes from one generation to the next unless its broken by the word of God.

No matter how educated you may be, college degrees can never remove a curse from you. So many educated people are under a curse of poverty, and that is why they look tattered. Academics is not a cure to spiritual problems, although it widens your understanding and knowledge. Hear this: Spiritual knowledge is supreme and divinely given, but academic knowledge is mental supplements that help you manage accurately certain information at place of work. Light operates on blessing principles, while a curse works on damaging blessings.

WHAT TO DO DURING DARKNESS OR TIMES OF TRIAL

Every trials in life respond to positive word of God. Therefore during trials or tribulation your response make all the difference.

It's written:

> [20] But as for you, ye thought evil against me; but God meant it unto good, to bring to pass, as it is this day, to save much people alive. Genesis 50. 20 (kJV)

When you experiencing trials position your mind positively and speak to the situation with right word of God. Whatever evil enemy planned against you will turned upon them. Don't ever think of committing suicide, when you respond with the spirit of God's sword, enemy will flee.

For thus said the LORD to the house of Israel, 'Seek me, and ye shall live'. (Amos 5:4)

You must seek God with all your faith to conquer every battle of life.

O God, thou art my God; early will I seek thee: my soul thirsteth for thee, my flesh longeth for thee in a day and thirsty land, where no water is. (Psalms 63:1)

Seeking God early is as conquering the problem from the root, not at the stalk or leaf.

There are numerous things or spiritual steps you can take when you notice malfunctions around you; below are a few spiritual working guides you can undergo:

➢ **Keep your faith alive.**

In times of trials and serious tribulations or temptations, your faith in Christ Jesus must be unshakeable. It's understandable that in times of trials, people's faith could be shift to doubting the saving power of God's words.

The greatest mistake people do in times of trials or temptations is to stay away from the house of God. Don't run away *from* God, but run *to* God and remain under His saving grace. When you notice that you are experiencing a symptom of darkness, or you are under satanic attack and things are getting out of your control, wage war against your situation by speaking the words of God with unmovable faith.

> **Keep your hope on God's words.**

It's normal for people to lose hope in critical situations or terrible problems. The children of God are not just people but peculiar and anointed messengers of the gospel of Christ. We are full of hope, no matter what the situation may be.

Hope for the best when situations turn for the worse. People with living hope turns hopeless situations into glorious testimonies. Hope draws us near to miracles; it brings God's attention into our matter.

Do you know that your negative thinking in times of trials can actually wash away your hope completely?

Negative words during trials are like erosion that has full force to wash away your hope; once erosion is not controlled, checked, or prevented, it will wash away good and bad crops from your farmland. Also, negative thinking or foolish attacks or criticising the word of God when you are facing storms of life could wash away your miracles.

> **Make the best use of your potentials.**

When you are confused in the midst of your problems, or when you lack the ability to be in control of temptations, trying times will mostly kill your potential.

Every potential in you will vanish. To be honest with you, I was once a victim. In the midst of my storms, I found myself taking advice from people I advised or counseled in the church. My leadership potentials started vanishing away because I stopped reading my Bible.

My attention was drawn away from the word of God to physically solving the problem. Suddenly, I realised that I am not at my best. So I started reading my Bible and engaged in fasting and prayer, then I became much stronger in faith than I was before.

No matter what comes my way, no matter the scandals, I am very organised and focused. Nobody knew in our church then that I was battling with my leadership quality. You must not lose your potentials. It will help you be in total control.

➤ **Fasten your fasting and prayer belt.**

Fasting is what most of today's Christians find difficult to do. I wonder where some Christians read in the Bible that fasting is for people of old or Jesus Christ was exempted us from fasting. No matter how educated you may be, you can't avoid trials or temptation.

The faster ways to come out of serious trials is through fasting and prayers. However, prayer alone is not enough; only water in the pot cannot be called a soup. Never you say fasting is not compulsory. For every vibrant spirit-filled child of God, fasting will refresh your anointing powers. A reasonable person will not run after food when problems suddenly become your best friend.

➤ **Study the word of God often.**

The entrance of the word of God into your life will enlighten all darkness. The words of God are powerful and quick to eliminate pains, sufferings, trials, and tough problems or difficulties. Seek God early, not when the problem has destroyed your faith and hope. I am a witness to His grace in His words.

Darkness means no trace of escape or exit. But in lighting up your environment, you can easily escape or find an exit. Only foolish Christians will believe that the power of darkness is not the cause of their predicaments; they stay on a pitiful state for years.

If darkness has anything to do with our Christian life, Jesus Christ wouldn't have come as light for us. He would have just come as Jesus Christ.

He actually said, 'I am "the Light"'.

When you read the Bible, have an eye for detail on every sentence and letter and understand what you read. The spirit of the words will reveal to you the solutions to your trials.

> **Be available for God to use.**

You must be in the house of God to praise Him. Don't say because you are facing challenges, you don't have time to preach or counsel people or attend church services. You must not allow your personal problems to stop the work of God. 'Cast your burden upon Him, for He careth'. If you refuse to turn to Him and continue your duty in His house, you will not find solutions to what you are facing, and your enemies or problems will not turn away from hurting you.

Hanna was available in the Shiloh to serve God. The time of a miracle requires your availability.

Once the fire of the Holy Spirit's anointing power is ready, you must be available to receive it. Fuel in a gallon cannot explode or catch fire by itself, but once fire is close by or made available, expect flames of huge fire with thick smoke—miracles.

The blessings of God or His power to change situations is often heavily present in the house of God.

Not all situations you pray about in your bedroom. But you can pray about all situations in the house of God and be assured of a miracle.

Performance of the word of God requires your performance— your service to God in His house.

When you do not perform well by reading your Bible and meditating, you will not perform well in the examination day (times of trials). So what you get is the outcome of your poor performance.

Champions are geniuses, not jokers. They are made in the ring and not the backstage of life.

Successful people in the kingdom of God are not those who make excuses, but in all unfavourable weather conditions, they are available.

➤ **Look unto heaven for help, not at your trials.**

Your constantly looking at your problem does not make the problem to go away from you. Rather, it magnifies the problem. Never you forget that your physical eyes only have one friend—tears. Until you look straight to heaven, solution may be hard in view.

¹**I will lift up my eyes unto the hill from whence cometh my help**

²**My help cometh from the LORD; which made heaven and earth.**

³**He will not suffer thy foot to be moved: he that keepth thee will not slumber. (Psalms 121:1–3)**

Looking at your problems every second and every minute will only aggravate the situation and worsen it all the more; it kills your faith and washes away your hope of healing. Look heavenwards and receive help from God, your Maker, who never sleeps, not slumbers. The only available help people who are not strong in relationship with God gets during times of trials is 'deceiving help'. Those who are not in Christ will be first to show you kindness to lure you into more traps of the devil.

Brethren, everything called sadness, disease, sick children, joblessness, unhappiness, constant bad news or severe pains that you are passing through today are caused by the power of darkness in high places. Don't ever believe your medical doctor's reports, remember not all doctors are born-again Christians. As for them, nothing like spiritual attack but disease is normal and anybody can fall sick and die.

> ¹⁹ He is chastened also with pain upon his bed, and the multitude of his bones with strong pain:
>
> ²⁰ So that his life abhorreth bread, and his soul dainty meat.

²¹ His flesh is consumed away, that it cannot be seen; and his bones that were not seen stick out.

²² Yea, his soul draweth near unto the grave, and his life to the destroyers.

(Job33: 19 -22 KJV)

You must stage defense on every forces of darkness, pray against them at midnight with fasting. You will be shocked the way things will start to work for you. take that sickness in your body as an enemy, I mean every problems of your life must be seen as enemy and not normal because it happened to people you know. Never you say; I don't care. Command the problem out of your life in Jesus name. if you want to live a victorious life, you must take spiritual fight to the camp of your enemies at midnight when all powers will be active to operate. Do you know that Satan have his agents in everywhere? in the hospitals, schools, and our place of work. There are satanic doctors that kill for Lucifer, in government, devil use his agents to cause war here and there; making the world unsafe.

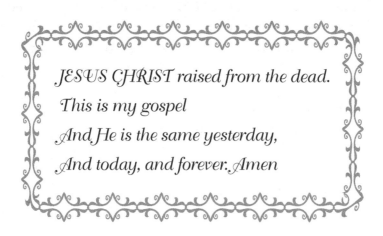

JESUS CHRIST raised from the dead.

This is my gospel

And He is the same yesterday,

And today, and forever. Amen

CHAPTER

Light in The Darkness

Christians are called light of God, and they are light in this dark world we live in.

I must say here that all people living in this dark world are children of God in a creative sense. Only real Christians are His children and are light to the Gentiles in a redemptive sense.

The day you realise that you are light, and you start living as light, darkness will not fellowship with you.

You cannot be light in darkness and still be darkness in light. You either chose to live as light in darkness and shine to glorify your Father in heaven or you chose to be darkness and live in darkness.

Christians are given light to live and shine; some of them still have interest in darkness like excess drinking, smoking, fornicating and partaking in family traditional practices. Thereby polluting the church of God, and work against spiritual growth.

They infect the weak in faith with immoralities, seduction, and discouraging spirits. They disorganise and disturb the peace of the saints. They cause division amongst brethren and distract them from hearing the word of God in the church services.

> **[14]You are the light of the world. A town built on a hill cannot be hidden. [15]Neither do people light a lamp and put it under a bowl. Instead they put it on its stand, and it gives light to everyone in the house. [16]In the same way, let your light shine before others, that they may see your good deeds and glorify your Father in heaven. (Matthew 5:14–16, NIV)**

Every believer is a light in this dark world, and nothing can stop them from shining. We are created by God to shine before others who live in darkness; Christians can easily chase away darkness from their domains, but darkness can never live in the light and survive it for a second.

There is darkness, and there is light. The greatest weapon darkness is afraid of is light because it exposes all hidden works of darkness.

Darkness reveals unbelief and light reveals faith in people.

The end of every darkness is called light.

When you say it is not your business to pray against the power of darkness and conquer them, it will soon be your daily business to eat medicine or go from one hospital to another. The power of darkness will come after you and deal with you mercilessly.

One major primary assignment of darkness is to stop you from shining as light.

So telling yourself that you have no business or time to pray against darkness shows that you have decided to remain in captivity for eternity.

> **For this is what the LORD has commanded us: 'I have made you a light for the Gentiles, that you may bring salvation to the ends of the earth'. (Acts 13:47)**

You are made light to rule over darkness and bring all souls in darkness to the *light*. Christians must not allow a single soul to remain in darkness.

In the previous chapter, we explained the effects of darkness. It is agreed that the common enemy of Christianity is darkness and its powers. The Bible confirmed that the last enemy was death. No good things are ever produced by darkness, and every Christian who aspire to live successfully on earth must prevail against all forms of darkness.

You could be residing in a dark world, but you must decide to live in light.

Your living in light will guarantee you victory while residing in the world of darkness as it is today. People of today prefer evil to good, darkness to light, wrong to right.

So Christians must make up their minds to stick to light at all times and let light remain in them. Running away from darkness shows that we are weak in faith, and the light in us in not glowing or shining.

Darkness hides good things from us and makes people to live in abject poverty for years.

But everything is exposed by light and becomes visible. It is only light that exposes hidden things of darkness; darkness can never expose light.

> **8For you were once darkness, but now *you are* light in the LORD. Walk as children of light 9(for the fruit of the Spirit *is* in all goodness, righteousness, and truth), 10finding out what is acceptable to the LORD. 11And have no fellowship with the unfruitful works of darkness, but rather expose *them*. 12For it is shameful even to speak of those things which are done by them in secret. 13But all things that are exposed are made manifest by the light, for whatever makes manifest is light. 14Therefore He says:**
>
> **'Awake, you who sleep,
> Arise from the dead,
> And Christ will give you light'. (Ephesians 5:8–14)**

When you are sleeping spiritually, you will never prevail against the power of darkness. No matter how smart you may be, you cannot work out of your challenges just like that.

You either wake up from your spiritual death and shine or you remain defeated by the power of darkness for the rest of your life. The problems of most people happened as a result of their inability to wake up spiritually and pray; instead, we run after perishable things, like cars or houses, leaving souls to walk into hell.

The most surprising thing I have seen in some Christians' homes is that they are afraid to pray dangerous prayers to send the devil packing. Rather, they pretend to be nice and Christianly. No matter how nice you may be, it cannot stop the devil from harassing you.

When you are living with crooks and wicked people, add the spirit of prayer to your life and be willing and ready to pray. The people whom you are nice to may not be nice to you, so pray them out of your way.

> **Do everything without complaining and arguing, that no one can criticize you. Live clean, innocent lives as children of God, shining like bright lights in a world full of crooked and perverse people. Hold firmly to the word of life; then, on the day of Christ's return, I will be proud that I did not run the race in vain and that my work was not useless. (Philippians 2:14–16)**

The easiest way to strengthen the devil is to be arguing that there is no power of darkness or demons anywhere. This world is full of crooked and perverted people who are specially trained by the devil to cause havoc. To shine in their midst requires absolute control of your spiritual life through fervent prayers.

Do you know that every family on earth have evil patterns? In some family, there's pattern of death that kill the family members, some, pattern of disease or delay and pattern of suffering. Everybody in the family surfers this evil patterns. If you come from such family or you marry from the family, the evil patterns will affect you unless you pray seriously against all evil patterns of your family and your spouse's family. I have seen men who are doing well in life and immediately after marriage they lost everything - lost their job, house, car, and business. Some cases I have handled, the couples are innocents and they are Christians.

The problem is from family pattern. It could be the family of the man or the wife, the enemy of the family will destroy every good things. The man will start to suffer from year to year without any meaningful results. The devil is a destroyer of progress and hope. No matter your educational status, you can never find a good job when this evil patterns are in operation.

How can we live in light while residing in a dark world?

❖ **Christians must shine their light by placing it in the most strategic places.**

Since we are created by light, and light was given us to shine in this world that is full of people and practices of darkness, Christians must choose the type of friends you want in your life or places you want to reside in. If you choose or place your light in a place where you cannot shine out, it may take you years to get results.

Always look for strategic places to shine your light.

> **[14]You are the light of the world. A town built on a hill cannot be hidden. [15]Neither do people light a lamp and put it under a bowl. Instead they put it on its stand, and it gives light to everyone in the house. [16]In the same way, let your light shine before others, that they may see your good deeds and glorify your Father in heaven. (Matthew 5:14–16, NIV)**

The lamp is put on its stand to give light to everyone. Once you position yourself in a strategic place, shining becomes easy. A wrong place can place you on a wrong side of life. Those who chose not to see anything wrong with the way they live live a life of slavery and complains.

I encourage you to shine as light to win lost souls to Christ. For you to be relevant on earth, shining as light must be your desire. There is a prize awaiting everyone who shines as light, so work hard for your prize by residing in light.

❖ **Avoid the temptation of sins that will hide your light.**

If anyone who is residing in this wicked and dark world wants to shine, he or she must avoid sin completely. Sin hides your light and prevents your light from shining. It is dangerous to fool around sins.

The devil, who planned the fall of the saints and the accusers of the brethren, work tirelessly to entice children of God with things, like worldly possessions and wealth, that will cause their fall into sin. Once you commit a sin and you did not confess it and ask forgiveness for it, the sin will destroy your glorious destinies, thereby giving the devil an opportunity to hijack your shining light and destroy your promising life and finally send you to dungeon.

Darkness goes after a believer's light to stop it from shining once the believer commits a sin.

You can live in light and shine continuously while residing in a dark world, but avoid doing things that those in the dark world love doing.

If you keep to righteousness and holiness, darkness will become irrelevant, and its fears will never bother you.

Those who never stay away from sins never stay close to God.

❖ **Christians must not partake in darkness activities but must expose them.**

Christians who partake in darkness activities while still going to the house of God are 'deceivers'. Their end is lost. That is why many Christians are in pain today because they refuse to expose their past engagements with darkness.

Never you bear false witness against the innocent. Expose darkness and its workers. Never you go into an agreement with darkness for any reason; it is a trap to set you up and later give you conditions that would make it difficult for you to expose them.

Some Christians have fallen victims of partaking in darkness activities.

They swore an oath never to expose their secrets 'til death. Such people I call unlearned because they don't read the Bible to understand that darkness have no power to save.

So many great men of God once lived in light. They shone in miracles, signs, and wonders. But because of their sudden interest in wealth, they partake in darkness activities to amass wealth and fame for themselves.

If you want to get involved in dubious things or partake in powers of darkness to suddenly get rich, be ready for calamities and gross darkness when the author of all sadness and pains, Satan, comes with his rewards.

There is no sudden wealth without the support of the devil, and in every sudden wealth, there is sudden death.

Christians, keep your slate clean at all times and expose the devil.

You cannot run your life race with people of the dark power because you are now a child of light.

> **Do not be yoked together with unbelievers. For what do righteousness and wickedness have in common? Or what fellowship can light have with darkness? What harmony is there between Christ and Belial? Or what does a believer have in common with an unbeliever? (2 Corinthians 6:14–15)**

In the churches today, believers are involved in gossiping, backbiting, scandals, secretly condemning the pastor's character and sermons, bearing false witness— these are works of darkness, not light. It is unfortunate that Christianity has been hijacked by immorality and disobedience.

What fellowship can light have with darkness? Expose the works of darkness if you know you are light.

❖ **Be careful of what you say to others.**

Let no evil or corrupting talks come out of your mouth. Only talks that are for building up others should come out of you. The words we speak are powerful. It can kill or save. The words that come out of our mouth can be used to judge our characters. Our words can make us shine or kill the chance of our shining. There are restless evil tongues and deadly poison.

> **But no man can tame the tongue. It is an unruly evil, full of deadly poison. (James 3:8, NKJV)**

When you know that your goal is to make it to heaven, and you want to remain the light of this world, mind what you say. Your tongue can put out the light of God in you, and it can also keep you shining. Since the tongue is restless, unruly, and full of deadly poison, we must learn how to use our tongue to speak kind words that will bring people to God's house, and when they come and see our light glowing, they will have a change of mind to follow God's ways and drop darkness activities.

> **Let no corrupt word proceed out of your mouth, but what is good for necessary edification, that it may impart grace to the hearers. (Ephesians 4:29, NKJV)**

When you allow darkness communication to proceed out of your mouth, you are giving rooms to questions like, does he really know that he's child of God? How can a child of God talk like the ways he talks? He goes about telling people about God and doing another thing. What kind of Christian is he? I don't think God called him. Never you allow people in the dark world rubbish your light because of what we say with our tongue. Speak like children of light.

Instances when people shine in this dark world we live in

❖ **Our Lord Jesus Christ**

> **And He was transfigured before them. His face shone like the sun, and His clothes became as white as the light. (Matthew 17:2, NKJV)**

❖ **The Shining Face of Moses**

> **Now it was so, when Moses came down from Mount Sinai (and the two tablets of the Testimony *were* in Moses' hand when he came down from the mountain), that Moses did not know that the skin of his face shone while he talked with Him. (Exodus 34:29, NKJV)**

❖ **Stephen's Face Shines**

> **And all who sat in the council, looking steadfastly at him, saw his face as the face of an angel. (Acts 6:15, NKJV)**

❖ **John the Baptist Shines**

> **He was the burning and shining lamp, and you were willing for a time to rejoice in his light. (John 5:35, NKJV)**

Christians shine for God.

> **Then Jesus spoke to them again, saying, 'I am the light of the world. He who follows Me shall not walk in darkness, but have the light of life'. (John 8:12, NKJV)**

> **Let your light so shine before men, that they may see your good works and glorify your Father in heaven. (Matthew 5:16, NKJV)**

Three fundamental questions we need to ask ourselves and answer before we accept the responsibility to shine in this dark world of corruption.

1. WHERE CAN CHRISTIANS SHINE?

❖ **Christians are to shine in 'the universe'.**

This is the world in which we all live, and it also refers to the world system that opposes Christians' faith and the work of Christ. Everyone forbids to love a perfect world where we are expected to shine to glorify God. (1 John 2:15–17) It is true that we are living in the world, but Christians are not to be involved in the evil and darkness activities that have become the way of everyone in the world today.

> ¹¹**Now I am no longer in the world, but these are in the world, and I come to You. Holy Father, keep through Your name those whom You have given Me, that they may be one as We** *are.*
>
> ¹⁵**I do not pray that You should take them out of the world, but that You should keep them from the evil one.**
>
> **(John 17:11, 15, NKJV)**

John 17:11 and 15 make clear that our universe is only safe for when we have Christ in our lives.

❖ **Christians are to shine in a 'crooked perverse generation'.**

> ¹³**From those who leave the paths of uprightness to walk in the ways of darkness;** ¹⁴**Who rejoice in doing evil,** *and* **delight in the perversity of the wicked;** ¹⁵**Whose ways** *are* **crooked, And** *who are* **devious in their paths. (Proverbs 2:13–15, NKJV)**

What a great spiritual and moral darkness that destroyed this world!

In everyone's mind, there are evil thoughts and a complete ignorance of God's light. The world would have been peaceful if man has not held his mind unto wrong thoughts and sold his soul to the devil through evildoing continually.

The moral darkness and spiritual ignorance is an indication of the wrong system put in place by Satan to increase the rate of divorce, drinking, gambling, sexual immorality, crimes, and drug addiction. God saw humans' end in this world, and it was not what He intended for man. Therefore, He sent us His son Jesus Christ to die for man and save man from destruction.

> **Then the LORD saw that the wickedness of man *was* great in the earth, and *that* every intent of the thoughts of his heart *was* only evil continually. (Genesis 6:5, NKJV)**

What the Lord saw in the Genesis 6:5 was true of this present generation; laziness and evil have become societal crops that grow in the soil hearts of everyone living on earth, a generation that killing of souls for money is normal, naked dressing a norm in the church, and harlotry or adultery happily embraced in the church to increase membership.

Christians no longer consider purity and holiness important but join the unbeliever to celebrate sins because they cannot bear or withstand hardship.

Our streets are littered with evil and the blood of the innocents flowing across the road into the gutters. Our places of worship are unhealthy to be called synagogue.

> **As it was in the days of Noah, so it will be at the coming of the Son of Man. (Matthew 24:37, NIV)**

It is in this crooked and depraved generation that we are to shine for the Lord; in public and in private, we must shine. Noah shone for God by doing what was pleasing to God.

2. HOW CAN CHRISTIANS SHINE?

> [12]Therefore, my dear friends, as you have always obeyed— not only in my presence, but now much more in my absence— continue to work out your salvation with fear and trembling,
>
> [13]for it is God who works in you to will and to act in order to fulfill his good purpose.
>
> [14]Do everything without grumbling or arguing, [15]so that you may become blameless and pure, 'children of God without fault in a warped and crooked generation'. Then you will shine among them like stars in the sky [16]as you hold firmly to the word of life. And then I will be able to boast on the day of Christ that I did not run or labor in vain. (Philippians 2:12–16, NIV)

Christians, as light bearers, must do everything in the house of God without grumbling, complaining, or arguing. Those who grumbled or argued with God never shine as stars.

In life generally, light in a lantern may be weak or ineffective because the wick needs attention or be replaced or the glass is smoky or dirty. The owner of the lantern or lamp will have to remove the glass, and wash it thoroughly; thereafter, clean the wick very well before putting on the lantern. The lantern will shine like a star in the sky. So are our lives. When sin makes us dirty and shining becomes difficult, we need the word of God to wash away our impurities so that we can shine amongst the wicked for Lord.

How can we shine?

❖ Avoid complaining or muttering

Complaining is a killer of people's miracles and destinies. Christians who find it difficult to live a Christian life without complaining will find it difficult to receive from God. Complains will make you sin against God. People who complain, naturally, are never satisfied with whatever is given to them. Do everything without grumbling and be blameless, then you will shine like a star amongst complainers. (verse 14).

> ²Now there was no water for the congregation; so they gathered together against Moses and Aaron. ³And the people contended with Moses and spoke, saying: 'If only we had died when our brethren died before the LORD! ⁴Why have you brought up the assembly of the LORD into this wilderness, that we and our animals should die here? ⁵And why have you made us come up out of Egypt, to bring us to this evil place? It *is* not a place of grain or figs or vines or pomegranates; nor *is* there any water to drink'. ⁶So Moses and Aaron went from the presence of the assembly to the door of the tabernacle of meeting, and they fell on their faces. And the glory of the LORD appeared to them. (Numbers 20:2–6, NKJV)

> And the people spoke against God and against Moses: 'Why have you brought us up out of Egypt to die in the wilderness? For *there is* no food and no water, and

**our soul loathes this worthless bread'.
(Numbers 21:5, NKJV)**

The people of Israel complained against God and against Moses because there is no water or food. The moment there is no food or money in the house, some people's faith gets weak, and they begin to speak against God. Why are people always seeking food, cars, and house than God's words? How can a Christian prefer food or water or earthly properties to eternal life? Are you demonically possessed by food? Such people demand for food or drinks anywhere they go.

Such people can never be respected or will not shine amongst the great but low profiles. Each time you argue or murmur against God, you are on the way out of His shining promises and glories. The unwise gossips men of God or children of light.

- ❖ Be blameless. (verse 15)
- ❖ Be completely trustworthy. (Daniel 6:4)
- ❖ Be pure. (verse 15)
- ❖ Be completely wholesome and sincere. (John 1:47 and 1 Peter 2:1)
- ❖ Be without fault. (verse 15)

Live in a way that we do not have to be corrected or chastened always by the Lord because of our sins.

- ❖ Hold out the word of life. (verse 16)

When you hold out the word of God, you are His active witness in preaching the gospel and demonstrating your faith in Christ Jesus. This can only be possible by a consistent life in Christ in season or out of seasons.

❖ Live in the light Christ. (verse 16)

The apostles chose to live by the light of Christ and the mighty works that were done through them that made them shine amongst people. Day by day, remain in the light of Christ; the world we are now does not want people to live in the light of God, so you must work out your salvation.

3. WHY SHOULD CHRISTIANS SHINE?

❖ **To glorify God the Father**

In the same way, let your light shine before others, that they may see your good deeds and glorify your Father in heaven. (Matthew 5:16, NIV)

The level of light you have in Christ and His shining glory in your life will determine the level of your glory to Him. To glorify your Father in heaven requires a Christ-filled life and a Holy Spirit-controlled life that make you glow before men and commend Him to them. We shine before the world and people to glorify God in heaven. It is your duty in this world to do everything to show Christ to the Gentiles and to shine His light in the life of men—this glorifies the Father in heaven.

❖ **To magnify our Lord Jesus**

I eagerly expect and hope that I will in no way be ashamed, but will have sufficient courage so that now as always Christ will be exalted in my body, whether by life or by death. (Philippians 1:20, NIV)

To magnify a thing is to make it appear bigger or greater, and Christians, by their shining witness of Christ to the Gentiles, magnify the Lord Jesus, just as lamps or lanterns magnify the light. The Lord appears bigger before the world. Therefore, let us magnify and exalt Him.

❖ To make the gospel great

> **30'He must become greater; I must become less'.**
>
> **31'The one who comes from above is above all; the one who is from the earth belongs to the earth, and speaks as one from the earth. The one who comes from heaven is above all. (John 3:30–31, NIV)**
>
> **He was the burning and shining lamp, and you were willing for a time to rejoice in his light. (John 5:35, NKJV)**

A lantern does not attract to itself, but it is the light that attracts.

Before you can shine in life, you must burn, sacrifice, and the brighter you want to shine in life, the more sacrifices are expected from you.

There can be no shining without burning, and there is no sacrifice without shining.

Our willingness to burn than the rest of the people will show that Christ is all and all in our lives.

John the Baptist allowed himself to decrease for Christ to increase. He was a burning and a shining lamp, yet he chose to allow Christ be above all in his life.

Those who never lost sight of burning and shining for Christ will always rejoice in the everlasting reward of the light. Your willingness to decrease for Him to increase will trigger His willingness to increase you so that you can glorify His Father in heaven.

❖ **To save the sinners**

> **⁸When I say to the wicked, 'O wicked *man,* you shall surely die!' and you do not speak to warn the wicked from his way, that wicked *man* shall die in his iniquity; but his blood I will require at your hand. ⁹Nevertheless if you warn the wicked to turn from his way, and he does not turn from his way, he shall die in his iniquity; but you have delivered your soul.**
> **(Ezekiel 33:8–9, NKJV)**

The prophet of God gives us a red warning on the repercussion of failing to save the life of sinners. To save our soul is to save the soul of sinners in the church and in the society. No matter how wicked people around us appeared, preach Christ to them.

We are to shine before men and women with the red light of warning, and we must constantly show the green light or maintain a consistent brightly-burning life of God. Our bright or green light that we keep will point sinners to the way of salvation and when they accept Jesus as Lord and Saviour. When we shine brightly amongst the sinners, it is an indication that we can win them to Christ because our burning life for Christ will transform their lives.

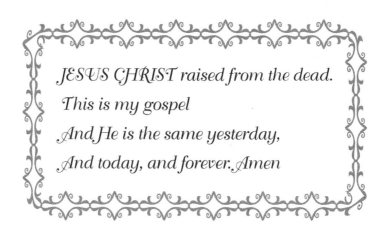

JESUS CHRIST raised from the dead.
This is my gospel
And He is the same yesterday,
And today, and forever. Amen

CHAPTER

9

Victory Over Darkness

The life is full of storms, challenges, and obstacles, and with our spiritual inexperience about life, we have a limited and infinite understanding of our infinite God.

Life is about victory over darkness completely. Some Christians misunderstand the meaning of darkness, and they pay little or no attention to the operational system of the power of darkness around them. They never like a church where the man of God speaks against satanic activities. Such people will never attend churches that cast out demons out of people or pray against the powers of darkness.

They feel that preaching against the powers of darkness and its agents is not proper. But they forgot that our Lord Jesus Christ spoke against demons and unclean spirits and did cast unclean spirits out of people.

Their unbelief about kicking out demons and unclean spirits out of people cause their early death.

They died simply because of unbelief that demons and unclean powers are not behind their problems. The need to worry about the power of darkness was not in them.

They justified their arguments by saying the gospel of Christ is about salvation and not about demonism, witchcraft, or dark powers. Their line of thought is that Christ has defeated all powers of darkness, and there is no point that we, the new covenant generation of grace, should bother ourselves with casting out devil.

Never you fall cheaply into this group of baby and blind Christians. If you don't consider praying against the power of darkness important, you will suffer many things in the hand of the devil.

The people who walk in darkness will see a great light; those who live in a dark land, the light will shine on them. (Isaiah 9:2)

If there is no darkness or dark land, Isaiah wouldn't have given us hope over darkness. 'The people who walk in darkness will see a great light'.

You can't just sit down and wait for victory over your situations; there are things you need to do that will guarantee you victory in life, no matter how tough the situation is.

There is no laboratory where chemical reactions or atomic combinations can provide you spiritual analysis of the demonic attacks on your life.

If you don't believe that the world was spiritually created and that man was spiritually appointed by God to rule over other creatures, including the devils and demons, you will never recognise the fact that you have spiritual duties to perform and you need to approach things spiritually for better performance.

Spiritual ignorance is when your unbelief has blinded your spiritual hearing and also blocked your spiritual antenna to the voice of the Holy Spirit. You are only ignorant of the vices of the devil, but the devil is not ignorant of your unlimited powers.

Satan only made you look unharmed, but underneath, he cleverly made your life twisted.

The following are some steps that the believer should take:

❖ **Understand your enemy.**

It is important that we understand our enemy. Understanding the enemy will help you terminate, disconnect, and respond swiftly. Quickly hit his base with the thunderbolt of God. If you are sick, and you went to the hospital, the doctor will run tests on the you, for he has to understand the nature of the sickness, and he has to know the means of transmission and to limit its spread. Thereafter, the doctor will quickly start treatment.

The devil is the enemy of Christians, and we need to fully understand him and deal with him aggressively through the word of God.

We need to know what he is able to do, his limitations, and the various ways in which he works.

The Bible says put on the full armor of God so that you can take your stand against the devil's schemes. (Ephesians 6:11) Different people with different problems and our problems requires different prayers to tackle it. Never you feel or accept that problems or sickness are normal because it happened to someone you know.

That someone you know is not you. You are a child of God to whom God has given victory over Satan and his works.

Brethren, never you accept things that other people out there suffered and accepted as normal or you believed in your heart that it can happen to anyone.

Be aggressive in prayers and read the word of God every time to understand the devil's tricks. Those who exhibit an I-don't-care behaviour or attitude remain on the list of pains. Satan takes advantage of those who are spiritually immature and are handicapped in prayers.

❖ **Be watchful at all times.**

> **Be sober, be watchful: your adversary the Devil, as a roaring lion, walks about, seeking whom he may devour. (1 Peter 5:8)**

Never you play into the devil's hand. Don't mingle with his agents. Stay away from all his activities. While you are isolating yourself from him and his agents, be watchful and be on guard against his attacks. Some Christians are careless and never thought that nobody can do them harm. When it is obvious that their enemy is their households, they pretend not to believed. Some will say, 'Pastor, how can my own mother or sister be my problem? How can my wife or husband plan to kill me?' Man of God, there is a mess-up somewhere.

There is nothing you can say to such people to believe you; in some cases, they stop fellowship.

What does it cost you to pray about the revelation and be watchful? Never you take the enemy for granted. The impacts of their evil on you may be devastated.

Be watchful, I say. In this world of money and wickedness, the devil is closer than the nose to the mouth.

❖ **Resist him when he attacks.**

The Bible tells us to resist the devil. Don't give the devil a breathing space.

Contain him with prayer and fasting. Bomb his strong house, where he hides his powers. I mean, his operational sites, like covens, hills, evil rocks, the sea, and everywhere he holds meeting, must be set ablaze completely.

> **Be subject therefore unto God; but resist the Devil, and he will flee from you. (James 4:7)**

Resist means to withstand or to stand your ground with faith and prayers. By standing our ground, Satan can be overcome. John wrote to believers:

> **I am writing to you, fathers, because you know Him who is from the beginning. I am writing to you, young people, because you have conquered the evil one. (1 John 2:13)**

No one folds his hand in battle and expected to be a hero. Neither did anyone is called a warrior by sitting comfortably at home while others were at the battle front.

In every warrior, there is a spirit of fighting; and in every winner, there is a skin of warrior on him. No warrior gives up, and no loser is called a winner. Resist the devil. Fight with everything at your disposal: prayers, fasting, sacrifice, soul-wining mission, praises, and above all, have high hopes of defeating the devil in your heart.

❖ **Work on your weak areas.**

Every human being has areas in their life in which they are vulnerable. Satan knows these areas. Consequently, the devil especially attacks the areas where Christians are weak. The Bible commands us not to give any opportunity to the devil, respond aggressively with dangerous prayers that rent apart mountains, and divide seas of problems, commanding the wave of the seas to stop. Arrest and incarcerate all witches in your areas and jail them in a bottomless pit of hell.

In any area you rent an apartment, build a house, or buy a home, there is a witch or an evil man or woman who is an evil press reporter. In every street, there is a witch or wizard that spies or monitors people's life. This evil spirits daily gather information about people's progress and report to their coven or altar. There is also international connectivity between your family witchcraft and witchcrafts in the area you are staying. I called them international witchcraft. Their duty is to gather information about everyone in the area or street and report to their headquarter, covens or altars of darkness where the stupid Lucifer will give order to torment the person.

Work on your areas of weakness; if it's prayer, rise at midnight and call all the witches in your area or street or zone to battle. Never you allow them to sleep or have a successful evil meeting. Call the Holy Ghost's fire upon them until they become uncomfortable to stay in your area. Disturb their meeting every night with dangerous prayers.

Don't be weak in faith or fasting. Do serious damage to all evil kingdoms by using the word of God, the spirit of the sword. Tear down kingdoms and set ablaze witch habitations.

Drop mass destructive missiles called Holy Ghost fire into satanic meetings or evil thrones in your area where you are living.

When you work on your weak areas, you will keep your areas safe, and fear will be no more.

Fear gives opportunity to the devil to do more wicked things and make it impossible for you to have victory over his works. Our fears that we may not be able to conquer evil's power actually empowered the devil to lord over us. Take the devil down through fasting and prayers. Take him down now, quick and fast! Christians who cannot fast for fourteen days, twenty-one days, thirty days, or forty days cannot do much. You must be a giant in faith and in fasting to be able to knock the devil down and paralyse all powers, visible and invisible. Don't rely on your power before you take on the devil. You can handle all witch powers and Lucifer powers; no power that Jesus's name that is in you cannot terminate or destroy.

❖ Avoid the same situations and mistakes.

Repeating one mistake over and over gives the devil the power to control and manipulate our plans, twist them, and frustrate all efforts of success.

Christians should avoid any situation that causes them to sin. They should separate themselves from the source of temptations and focus on the saving grace of God.

When you separate yourself from a particular sin or avoid repeating the same mistake, you will have victory over satanic powers that control your affairs.

You must separate morally and geographically by prayer.

Abstain from every form of evil. (1 Thessalonians 5:22)

Staying with evil people or living in an evil environment will encourage you to live a sinful life, and you cannot have interest of seeking for God or going to His house for prayers.

Every evil you find difficult to separate from will destroy your good goals in life and leave you in a pitiful situation. However, all victories are only temporary because temptation will always come as long as we are in these bodies. But when you remain in Christ Jesus and serve God only, He will take care of all your situations and mistakes of the past and give you a permanent victory over the devil. For He has conquered the devil and gave us victory over all evils.

❖ **Overcome the power of darkness by the blood of the Lamb.**

And they overcame him by the blood of the Lamb, and by the word of their testimony; and they loved not their lives unto the death. (Revelations 12:11)

Never you underestimate the power of darkness, but overcome the power of darkness by the blood of Jesus Christ. Remember to call the blood of Jesus Christ to help you overcome the devil.

Much more then, being now justified by his blood, we shall be saved from wrath through him. (Romans 5:9)

The only weapon the devil does not withstand is the blood of the Lamb. The wrath of power of darkness are best overcome and made harmless by the calling upon the blood of the Lamb.

There is a wrath of Satan in every sin he made us commit; you may not know, but there is devil wrath in every sin or temptation.

The devil gives people pretentious advice or blessings that look good, but later he adds sorrow to it, making people face his wrath, pain, or depression.

❖ **Remain as His redeemed.**

You are the redeemed of the Lord, so remain in Him, no matter what you are facing. He will redeem you from the hand of evil and wickedness. Wrath will not and can never be placed upon you nor your family or anything that belongs to you.

Let the redeemed of the LORD say so, whom he hath redeemed from the hand of the enemy. (Psalms 107:2)

For those who go to church and still participate on family tradition or community festival celebration, you can never overcome the devil or stand against darkness.

On the day of trial, winning the battle becomes difficult because you are part of the devil by participating in evil festival.

Do you know that most of the community festivals that some Christians involve themselves because they want to be a voice in their village are traps that the enemy uses to enter into them and establish or stage attack on them?

I heard a story of a successful businessman in Europe who did well in business one certain year. After he completed his own house in the village, he was invited to a village festival celebration, and they conferred on him a title of 'RED CAP'.

The long story cut short, on his arrival in Europe, the man died of a strange attack.

He could not sleep in the house he laboured to build with his hard-earned money. Remain in God as His redeemed, and He will protect you from all evil and arrows of the day and of the night.

There shall no strange god be in thee; neither shalt thou worship any strange god. (Psalms 81:9)

Be ye not unequally yoked together with unbelievers: for what fellowship hath

> **righteousness with unrighteousness? and what communion hath light with darkness? (2 Corinthians 6:14)**

Brethren, have nothing to do with your village festival or community title of red cap or any fetish things. The end of such chieftaincy title is death.

> **But if we walk in the light, as he is in the light, we have fellowship one with another, and the blood of Jesus Christ his Son cleanseth us from all sin. (1 John 1:7)**

❖ **God's dwelling power is in us.**

Those who dwell in the secret place of the Lord enjoy His secret power, and they don't fear anything because no strange gods can make them afraid.

Dwell in God completely, my brethren. There is no safe place, except the canopy of the Lord. Those involved in double-worshipping, one leg in the house of house and the other leg in the covens of wickedness, are trading with their lives, and on the day of storms, the devil will abandon them. I have seen a man who was an elder in the church and also a grandmaster of a fraternity. When he died, there was a great confusion. As the pastor was about to pray on the dead body, the fraternity members came on full regalia and took away the coffin with the dead body. The place was thrown into confusion. What an embarrassment!

You cannot hide your evil forever. Why not come out of secret cults, you as a pastor or elder or bishop that is ignorantly involved in fetish powers? Come out now. I say come out now and be saved and receive the power to overcome darkness.

Run to God for safety and save your souls and all members of your family. Never you run to darkness to overcome darkness. You cannot sleep on the devil's bed and then destroy the devil.

> **Know ye not that ye are the temple of God, and that the Spirit of God dwelleth in you? (1 Corinthians 3:16)**

> **There shall no strange god be in thee; neither shalt thou worship any strange god. (Psalms 81:9)**

> **Be ye not unequally yoked together with unbelievers: for what fellowship hath righteousness with unrighteousness? and what communion hath light with darkness? (2 Corinthians 6:14)**

You must reexamine any invitation by your friends to attend an occasion that is not in the house of God or crusade or gathering of children of God and the consequences of the invitation to your life before accepting to attend.

In every unrighteousness invitation, there are unrighteousness activities that lead to sin.

SPIRITUAL PRINCIPLES TO OVERCOME POWERS OF DARKNESS.

❖ **If God is against it, so am I.**

> **[19]The acts of the flesh are obvious: sexual immorality, impurity and debauchery; [20]idolatry and witchcraft; hatred, discord, jealousy, fits of rage, selfish ambition,**

dissensions, factions [21]and envy; drunkenness, orgies, and the like. I warn you, as I did before, that those who live like this will not inherit the kingdom of God. (Galatians 5:19–21, NIV)

The above Bible quotes means

Galatians 5:19–21: 'Now the works (deeds) of the flesh (humans) are manifest (revealed), which are these; Adultery (sex with other than your wife), fornication (sex outside of marriage), uncleanness (sexual impurity), lasciviousness (sexual excess), Idolatry (things in your life that are more important than God), witchcraft (sorcery), hatred, variance (causing strife or discord), emulations (being jealous), wrath (sinful anger), strife (selfish ambition), seditions (dissentions), heresies (organised divisions or cliques), Envying, murders, drunkenness, reveling (excessive eating) and such like: of the which I tell you before, as I have also told you in time past, that they which do such things shall not inherit the kingdom of God'.

The Bible is full of passages that indicate behaviours that God is against. God asked us to avoid things He does not like.

The word of God warns us that participating in certain behaviour will bring sorrow, pain, and punishment and can lead to our death.

Everyone reading this book has seen that a certain behaviour or lifestyle is the reason many people are in serious painful situation today; this is true in not only our own lives, but also in the lives of many people, including Christians.

If you sow a destructive behaviour, you will reap destruction in your life.

Whatsoever a man sows, he shall reap. You cannot be sexually dressed to church and expect you to pray against sexual demons. Only your dressing has shown that you are spreading sexual appetites in the church.

If God's intention was to warn us of what is, what is not, how to get and how to stay right on his path, then He gives us new behaviour through the Holy Spirit to look like Him and do things as He would have done. Christians who want to overcome the devil must keep to this line of principle: 'If God is against it, so am I'.

❖ **Every sin begins in our hearts.**

⁹The heart _is_ deceitful above all _things,_ And desperately wicked; Who can know it? (Jeremiah 17:9, NKJV)

²³Above all else, guard your heart, for everything you do flows from it. (Proverbs 4:23, NIV)

Before we all came to Christ, there are certain things we tried to overcome in our lives like sexual addictions, drinking, or smoking. These things happened to us because of the place we go or find ourselves in. We would spend hours upon hours drinking with friends, smoking cigarettes, and discussing many endless desires, like to sleep with ladies or boys who are new in town. Does this sound familiar to you? This type of lifestyle has not helped anyone be successful in life but destroyed glorious destinies.

> ¹¹**And have no fellowship with the unfruitful works of darkness, but rather expose** *them.* ¹²**For it is shameful even to speak of those things which are done by them in secret.**
> **(Ephesians 5:11–12, NKJV)**

The above Bible verses remind us not to fellowship with the unfruitful works of darkness but rather reprove or expose them. For it is a shame even to talk about those things done in secret. Our sins of the past must be forgotten. To boast about them or discuss them openly shows that you are still interested in your past life, and even now, you are not ready for change. Such people need spiritual help to overcome the powers of darkness.

Once you are born again, you have nothing to do with darkness names you were once called by your friends. Distance yourself from thinking about help from your old friends who are into Satanism, but pray against their wrath and destroy their arrows completely through the blood of Jesus Christ.

Constant meditation (thinking) on our desire to fulfil a fleshly lust will ultimately lead to acting out our desire. If we're fortunate to avoid it physically, we will seldom avoid it mentally.

> **For as he thinketh in his heart, so is he . . .**
> **(Proverbs 23:7)**

For me to avoid the seemingly-unending desire to fulfil my desire to feed my addiction, I needed to discipline myself to avoid talking and thinking about it in a desirous way. By thinking about it, I was actually making it easy for myself to do wrong.

But put ye on the LORD Jesus Christ, and make not provision for the flesh, to fulfill the lusts thereof. (Romans 13:14)

You see, the heart can accustom itself to sin. An act that once seems terrible and undeniably wrong, by contemplating on it too often, becomes attractive.

Keep thy heart with all diligence; for out of it are the issues of life. Proverbs 4:23

Everything I ever searched for in life—the important issues of life: love, joy, peace, happiness, friendship, financial Freedom—were always withheld from me during my times of sinful life. Why was that? Because the important things of life are given by God, and He never entrusts them to those who do not work hard (diligent) to keep (guard) their hearts from being hardened from the deceit of sin. Remember, before you ever do it, think it over. I mean the consequences.

❖ **It is easier to keep your heart clean from evil than to clean it after it has been defiled.**

A prudent man foreseeth the evil, and hideth himself: but the simple pass on, and are punished. (Proverbs 22:3, NKJV)

²⁷ Can a man take fire to his bosom, And his clothes not be burned?

²⁸ Can one walk on hot coals, And his feet not be seared? (Proverbs 6:27–28, NKJV)

When a wise man sees trouble coming from afar, he will keep himself, but the foolish will say there is nothing that the ground cannot contain, and he will perish in his own foolishness. You cannot see fire coming and say it is water. Most Christians never see confession of sins to one another as a weapon to silence the devil and free oneself from guilt.

I used to tell my congregation that there are no sins I may mistakenly commit or fall into it that I will not tell my wife or confess it to the church. If I can commit it, I can confess it. Why? The devil always does spiritual judgement checks on believers.

If you know you cannot be bold to confess any temptation you fell into, don't fall into it. Don't be deceived that pastors or men of God cannot sin; this is a lie. We are flesh and blood, but His grace is our power over sins.

Keep your home, and mostly your heart, clean from been defiled. It may be difficult to clean it pure when it has been defiled.

Avoid quarrel in your home by cleaning your heart from what the devil may use against you before you start looking for friends or uncles to settle matters in your marriage.

Oh, what a truth this is! When my wife and I were first married, I had quite a lot of lessons to learn. I was an adult, yet not all things I know how to do. I was not accustomed to cleaning up bathroom after washing myself; as matter of fact, and it's the truth, I was not brought up in township bathroom but raffia palm bathroom that needed not to be cleaned after use. I had to learn in a hard way to keep my marriage happy.

My favourite meal was *garri*, an African meal, and my wife too have to learn how to make it for me. So we started learning new things about married life. Surprise! Sometimes my wife would refuse to prepare it because of the energy required to turn the *garri* on the pot. I was forced to teach her, and she became a professional and a better cook. We never had any issues in our marriage again. I can humbly say my wife taught me most things I did not receive from my mother because of my background. Kudos to Mama. Many men overlook the cleaning of the bathroom, making of the bed in the morning, cooking for the family, and putting dirty clothes of your wife or children in the washing machine. Have you considered how your wife will feel when she arrives home and finds everything looking nice and arranged?

A responsible man will not ask his wife when she will clean up the house.

BIG MISTAKE. Your first fight just began. I learned a valuable lesson the first day my wife corrected me on how to clean the bathroom mirror. After an hour of mopping the bathroom floor and cleaning the mirror, I learned it is easier to keep a kitchen or bedroom clean than to clean it after it has been messed up for too long.

When you overstay with a dirty environment, you will look like the environment, and unless someone corrects you, you will never see dirt as harmful to your spiritual life. Living in a clean environment is not about enlightenment or education but habit. I was enlightened and educated, but I was messing up our bathroom; leaving everything for my wife to keep clean was my greatest mistake. Christians are not cautious of the danger of a dirty environment. You may say I can afford a house help. Why should I or my wife bother to keep the house clean? You are wrong!

What will your wife remember you for at her private time? Men, listen, women count on little things than a bulk of money. Ask your wife about it.

This is the same truth we are taught in the Bible. Over and over, we are faced with examples of people who chose to associate with sin, with hopes that it would not lead them to a sinful condition. Lot was a righteous man (2 Peter 2:8), yet he chose to associate with ungodly men (Psalms 1:1a). He had day-to-day contact with sin (Psalms 1:1b), and he allowed the people around him to decay into moral wickedness with no good use for God (Psalms 1:1c). Yes, Lot's life was ultimately spared by God. However, he in no way prospered (Psalms 1:3). The last we heard of him, he is getting drunk and committing terrible sins (Genesis 19).

How can this mistake be avoided in your life? Follow these two simple verses:

> **A prudent man foreseeth the evil, and hideth himself: but the simple pass on, and are punished. (Proverbs 22:3)**

> **Can a man take fire in his bosom, and his clothes not be burned? Can one go upon hot coals, and his feet not be burned? (Proverbs 6:27–28)**

Remember: If you do what you've always done, then you will be what you've always been.

To avoid terrible things from happening in our future, do the right things *now*!

❖ **It is difficult to fight a fleshly appetite by indulging in it.**

James 1:14–15

Disregarding this principle has caused such great pain and failure for many years. It is also this very same principle that God will bring to our remembrance every time we feel like indulging in any fleshly desire. This principle has done more to discourage the desire to wander than any of the others.

If the truth be known, the failure to recognise and apply this principle to our lives is usually at the core of every besetting sin.

An appetite is a dangerous thing. If disciplined, it can be controlled. If not, it can control an individual. God has given each of His children the power to control our appetites. The need for food, drink, and sexual satisfaction are all God-given legitimate needs. However, Satan will twist them into lusts that, when coupled with enticement, lead to a life of sin and spiritual and sometimes physical death (James 1:14–16).

Remember the old commercial that advertised Benson & Hedges cigarettes?

The advertisement falsely stated that 'they satisfy'. Well, if this were true, then we could all smoke one Benson & Hedges cigarette, and our appetite would be satisfied, and we would never need to indulge that appetite again. The truth is that Benson & Hedges cigarettes, as do all cigarettes, never satisfy you.

An appetite created with indulgence will only intensify that indulging, and any fleshly appetite only makes you stronger and not weaker. Many people developed the habit of smoking because of this—to feel stronger and forget their sorrow. The truth is that cigarette kills your strength slowly and eventually sends you too early to the grave.

Not too long ago, I listened to a documentary on starving children in the third world. My heart was broken as the narrator explained that though the children were starving, they do not feel the hunger pains that we feel right before dinnertime. Rather, they have suppressed their appetite for so long that their starvation is not accompanied with the pain of hunger.

It is the same way with any fleshly desire that we struggle with. Be it cigarettes, drugs, alcohol, overeating, adulterous thoughts, pornography, gambling, or any other crippling appetite, if we do not feed it or do not give in to it, it will die. The only way to destroy the appetite is to starve your appetite with God's words, fasting and prayer. Do you know that there is a demonic power behind anything that you find difficult to stop and it becomes appetite? This represents our reality.

So the next time you feel that urge to indulge in a sinful fleshly desire, resign yourself to just 'skip that meal'. When you skip a meal, you will see that after a few minutes or hours, you have lost your appetite for that meal. You may not skip every meal, but eventually, your desire will starve itself to death, and the hunger will be gone. Don't let the devil tell you if you just have one more cigarette or just one more drink or one more chocolate bar, you will be satisfied.

He that loveth silver shall not be satisfied with silver; nor he that loveth abundance with increase: this is also vanity. (Ecclesiastes 5:10)

❖ **Little compromises lead to great disasters.**

So many new coverts and friends of the ministry have asked me questions like this: 'Pastor Emmanuel, I have stayed away from my old friends, I have stopped acting the way I used to, I even go to church at least once a week, but I still end up engaging in my addiction. How do I stop this old habit?'

Believers often ask such difficult questions with no easy answers during Bible teaching, but when you love God and care for the addicted person, they easily drop their habit.

Our ministry have seen men and women smoking and addicted to alcohol, yet I did not rebuke them but showed them love, and in some serious cases, I even made such people workers in the church, some Bible teachers, and within a short time, the word of God they read and taught the congregation changed them completely.

Today many are pastors and are doing great things in the kingdom of God. The secret of their changed lives was that they do not compromise or try to hide their old lifestyle. I know of one. One of my spiritual sons way back then, before he starts to teach Bible class, would ask the church to pray for him to stop smoking, and truly, the word he taught changed him.

> **No one can serve two master; for either he will hate the one and love the other or else he will be loyal to the one and despise the other. You cannot serve God and mammon. (Matthew 6:24)**

To avoid compromise in our faith, consistency in obedience and faith is required of us. Once you are faithful in small things, you can expect God to commit bigger things into your hands. However, inconsistency in little things makes us fail in life as Christians. God is looking for those who are hungry for little start and are faithful with the little blessings. God loves little things, and then He enlarges them into an overflowing pool of blessings. What determines your fruitful life is your little start and your consistent appreciation of God. Little things we often drop off the basket are what determines your master. The devil is a greedy man and never wants little things or never cares to follow the path of consistency that leads to great achievements.

You cannot serve God and earthly lust. You will have no choice but to love one and hate the other. The more you are unfaithful to God, the more you are inconsistent with man. Your ways will always be crooked. The more you do for God, the more you will learn to love Him, and the more you will be eager to do for man.

Those who serve mammon never avoid cutting corners in business, and they are authors of lies. They never help anyone without adding their own percentage.

Not only that, they will still collect more from you as if they are doing you a favour. The satisfaction of the flesh is the reason why some Christians have lost their holiness. I once told a friend of mine in Nigeria that it is difficult for anyone living in Nigeria to live a holy life. You can't live in Nigeria without bribery, and the few righteous ones are not recognised in the society because everyone on the street is a lover of money and promoter of atrocities. They want to make money regardless of what the innocent people feel. It is not only in Nigeria that the culture of showoff lifestyle is dominant but also in the whole world. This makes the world unsafe to live in and unhealthy for holiness. Man has suddenly become fearless and crazed for sudden wealth, and those who are called Christians have joined the decaying system. They compromised their faith for wealth and power. The day you welcome compromise into your faith, disasters become your offspring. Look at the streets.

You will see people who cut corners in business or in government. Their end is disgraceful and painful. Why do we love God? Because He first loved us! Don't fall for the trick of the devil. Life is more than the money, cars, and houses you kill or steal to acquire.

Let this word of God be in your heart if you really want God's blessings in your home or business.

> **You shall not cheat your neighbor, nor rob him. The wages of him who is hired shall not remain with you all night until morning (Leviticus 19: 13 NKJV)**

❖ **Those who do not love God will not help you to serve God.**

> **[18]Therefore the Jews sought all the more to kill Him, because He not only broke the Sabbath, but also said that God was His Father, making Himself equal with God. [19]Then Jesus answered and said to them, 'Most assuredly, I say to you, the Son can do nothing of Himself, but what He sees the Father do; for whatever He does, the Son also does in like manner. [20]For the Father loves the Son, and shows Him all things that He Himself does; and He will**

**show Him greater works than these, that
you may marvel'. (John 5:18–20, NKJV)**

**Through patience a ruler can be persuaded,
and a gentle tongue can break a bone.
(Proverbs 25:15, NIV)**

Soft words of those who do not know God will lure you into
sin and break your future into pieces. Be careful!

**If ye were of the world, the world would
love his own: but because ye are not of
the world, but I have chosen you out of
the world, therefore the world hateth you.
(John 15:19)**

Will my old friends in the world want anything to do with me
now that I am a Christian?

That was the question I asked myself many years ago after I
gave my life to Jesus.

It wasn't long before I found the answer. If I acted like them,
they would accept me. But if I acted like Christ, they would
reject me.

I struggled to determine the correct path. I wanted Christ in
my life, but I also wanted my old friends in my life. If I break
my ties with my worldly friends, I would lose opportunities I
enjoyed with them. So I tried to live as a child of God while
hanging out with the devil's kids. As you would expect, more
often than not, they would tempt me to do the things that I
did not want to do anymore. Eventually, I would give in, and
fall back into the life of sin.

It was at this time God showed me why misery loves companionship. If I lived right and remained right, my old friends would feel guilt and shame for their behaviour. But if I lived wrong, they would say to me that Christ has no effect on a personal life.

The guilt for their lifestyle would be removed and they would lay the snare (temptation) and wait for me to fall back into sin.

Lay not wait, O wicked man, against the dwelling of the righteous; spoil not his resting place. (Proverbs 24:25)

They would work hard to lure me back into the world as they wanted to see that my Christian life doesn't work. God forbid.

As we said in one of the services, look for people who love God to help you to serve God. As a child of God, you are not permitted to hang out with those who hate God. It is dangerous.

Your civilisation is not enough to overcome life battles. No!

The law of sowing and reaping would kick in, and they would find themselves at the bottom. Those who do not love God, when they encounter problems, would not look to their friends who did the same things. Rather, they would call on men of God to deliver them from troubles.

One day a brother in Christ came to me and asked me, 'Pastor, how I wished I could be simple like you'.

I told him, 'Brother, Jesus is my only wealth on earth and in heaven, so I am not in any competition with man to acquire the whole world. My wealth is the souls I won for Jesus Christ'.

This brother was amazed because my changed life was real. This real and simple life has earned me respect.

Do you know that in church and in town, you can't know that am a pastor unless somebody tells you in spite of the meekness and servant character I developed? It led to ministry prosperity and happiness. Just like the Bible promises in Psalms 1:1–3, 'Blessed (or happy) is the man that walketh not in the counsel of the ungodly, nor standeth in the way of sinners, nor sitteth in the seat of the scornful (listens to critical people). But his delight is in the law of the Lord; and in his law doth he meditate day and night. And he shall be like a tree planted by the rivers of water, that bringeth forth his fruit in his season; his leaf also shall not wither; and whatsoever he doeth shall prosper'.

People who do not love God, if they made you great, they will bring you down when you refuse to be loyal till the end. Never should you be unequally yoked with unbelievers and people who hate God. They will go the extra mile to drag your blessings and eventually kill you to inherit everything you laboured for.

Don't forget: *Those who do not love the Lord will not help you serve God.*

❖ Your sinful habits do hurt those who follow you.

Have you ever wondered if anybody cared? Have you ever thought about trying something drastic to get yourself noticed? 'Maybe then they would know I needed their help', you might say.

The devil, the father of all lies, would lie to you that no one is watching or caring for you. So nobody is affected by your sinful behaviour.

Since the beginning of the world, the devil is in business of deceiving people, and he has succeeded in deceiving many into believing that our behaviour does not affect others or hurt or damage ourselves.

❖ **Examples of Great People the Devil Deceived and They Fell**

➢ **Eve**

The devil deceived Eve that the forbidden tree is not harmful but will make her be like God. Little did she know that her sin would then be shared by her husband, which, in turn, would lead to the fall of man and woman. She didn't also know that a curse would be placed on herself and her husband and all generations yet unborn.

It's true that you may commit a sin alone. However, you cannot stay alone without associating or interacting or getting engaged in a relationship. Your sin will surely rub on anyone who have contact with you. Your bad habits affect others, and they may not know you have bad habits in the past that are living in your body cells as sickness.

➢ **Lot**

The devil deceived Lot. Not realising that having day-to-day contact with sinners was damaging to his family, he stubbornly left his homeland. His lack of leadership over his family led to the death of his wife and uncontrolled behaviour by his daughters and himself.

Our daily contact with people of bad characters has caused us painful, unforgettable lessons in life. Know who you follow so that anyone who will follow you will not regret.

> **David**

The devil deceived David. Little did King David know that if he stayed in his palace from battle that he would not suffer a temptation that would lead to adultery.

The consequence of his sin was the woman would lose her husband to a plot of murder and her newborn son would die. Over and over in the scripture, we see that sinful behaviour has a profound effect on those who follow us.

The position we occupy in life makes people follow us. Have we led our followers into deep regret and painful life? If you were to die today, would you have one thousand people at your funeral? Most people would like to think so because they thought their followers would follow them even to the grave. Only twenty out of one thousand would attend your funeral.

In the funeral of a bad man, only few people like him attended. These are the people your sinful habit affected negatively. You may not feel the pain of your sin anymore because you are dead, but your followers feel the pain more. When they look around the funeral ground, only evil men like them are present. They may not say to anyone what you said to them that made them follow you, but they would think in their heart that they wish, if it's possible, to find the courage to accept Jesus Christ.

For none of us liveth to himself, and no man dieth to himself. (Romans 14:7)

Your life affects others in the same way as your. Choose today how you want your life to affect others. Let your life have a profound effect of good on others. No matter the cost, no matter the sacrifice, make the choice today. Your good habits will help those who follow you.

Choose to read your Bible. Choose to talk to God in prayer. Choose to preach about Jesus Christ to someone today. Choose today to be helpful to those who come to the house of God. Choose today to make a difference in the lives of your congregation, the lives of your community, a difference in the Kingdom of God.

Choose Jesus Christ and follow Him.

➤ Judas Iscariot

I noticed that there are two things that a man likes that the devil kills with: (a) money and (b) woman or sex

When the only language in the mouth is money and how to catch babes in town, you are in a devil's workshop. There are some people, even Christians, that nothing they will ever do for you is free, but they will be calling God in the process of duping their fellow Christians. Satan is always roaming about the streets, looking for those who sit down with bottles of alcoholic drinks or beers and busily talking about women they caught up and slept with. This is the set of people that voted for the devil to rule the world.

Look around you, and you will see examples of people money and women or sex destroyed. Any woman who loves money will always experience late marriage, and when they eventually get married, they do two things: (a) cheat on their husband and (b) divorce when their needs are not met.

The closer you are to money, the closer you are to the devil. The devil likes every man who likes women and money. You cannot be a friend to the devil unless you are a permanent friend to sins.

Judas sold the owner of his life, Jesus Christ, for money. When you cannot learn from example of people around you who failed woefully, you are a graduate of poverty from the school of satanism.

To ruin one's life requires a complete loyalty to the devil. Those who wait for a push before they repent never escape the whip of the devil. Sometimes they never live to tell the story.

Many great Christians have gone to hell because of the race to make money overnight; they are often called harmer, the guy don harmer! Meaning, he has made money suddenly. If the business deal between Judas and the elder did not backfire, other disciples would have envied his sudden wealth.

❖ **It is difficult to fight a fleshly temptation with fleshly weapons.**

> **[3]For though we walk in the flesh, we do not war according to the flesh. [4]For the weapons of our warfare *are* not carnal but mighty in God for pulling down strongholds, [5]casting down arguments and every high thing that exalts itself against the knowledge of God, bringing every thought into captivity to the obedience of Christ. (2 Corinthians 10:3–5)**

The truth about our life is that life is a continuous praying and keeping our faith alive. Temptations are traps laid by the devil for the Christians to fall into and lose their faith in God. The weapon that is intended to curb our stubborn habits and inappropriate behaviour will not be the weapon to cure our afflictions. Every battle in our life starts from inside of us.

The battle is inside of us, and that is why our Lord Jesus Christ has chosen to take up residence in our lives. Since the battle of life is spiritual, and it starts operating or fighting us from inside, we cannot win such battle with a fleshly or worldly weapon.

> **You are of God, little children, and have overcome them, because He who is in you is greater than he who is in the world. (1 John 4:4, NIV)**

It is simple to believe but hard to apply. Whenever we have a stubborn thought, we must cast it down. It is our responsibility to protect our hearts with all diligence because out of the heart are the most important issues in life.

If there is going to be any good or anything worth commending come out of our lives, we must first concentrate on things that are true, honest, just, lovely, pure, and of good report. (Philippians 4:8) To avoid a habitual action or reaction to your negative thoughts, you must cast down the thought and bring your mind to obedience to Christ. You will have a lot of help with this, you see, because it says in 1 John 4:4, 'Ye are of God, little children, and have overcome them: because greater is he that is in you, than he that is in the world'.

The world has nothing to offer you in your quest for recovery. You can believe what you are reading, or you can try the world yourself. But with Christ, all things are possible if you only believe.

❖ **We lose our freedom to the devil when we give in to temptation.**

Isaiah 55:7

When we first take hold of a vice, it is extremely pleasurable. At times it may seem to be the only time we feel happy, the only time we experience any comfort in our lives. However, the Bible warns in Proverbs 20:17, 'Bread of deceit is sweet to a man; but afterwards his mouth shall be filled with gravel'. You can clearly see that while deceitful and wrong actions may bring temporary pleasure, afterwards, it leaves a very bad taste in your mouth. The consequences for your behaviour then belong to God.

> **Stolen waters are sweet, and bread eaten in secret is pleasant. But he knoweth not that the dead are there; and that her guests are in the depths of hell.**
> **(Proverbs 9:17–18)**

No matter how much enjoyment we may receive from our stubborn habit or addiction, we can be sure that the consequences are never worth it.

We must realise that God is watching us. He watches every single thing we do.

> **For the ways of man are before the eyes of the LORD, and he pondereth all his goings.**
> **(Proverbs 5:21)**

That word 'ponders' means to weigh or consider. What does He consider?

He considers the proper actions that should be taken against our behaviour to bring a proper reaction from us. His desire is for repentance and dependence on Him rather than on some vice that only bring temporal relief. Look at the warning that is given in the very next verse and ask yourself if you are in this position: 'His own iniquities shall take the wicked himself, and he shall be holden with the cords of his sins'. (verse 22)

This verse clearly indicates that once we grab hold of a wicked vice, it will begin to wrap itself around us. At the beginning, we may be able to get out of its hold, but eventually, the cord around us will tighten, and we will be held in bondage with the cords of our sin. Oh, how did this happen to me! Next is the important warning to those of us who struggle to fight back: 'He shall die without instruction; and in the greatness of his folly he shall go astray'. (verse 23)

This consequence (going astray, which leads to a premature physical and spiritual death) cannot be monitored by us. It is determined by God. Until that unfortunate time that we experience this untimely demise, we will have experienced consequences that are designed to bring us back to God. The cure is very simple and is recorded in Isaiah 55:7: 'Let the wicked forsake his way (1), and the unrighteous man his thoughts (2): and let him return unto the Lord (3) and he will have mercy upon him; and to our God, for he will abundantly pardon'.

We need God's mercy (unmerited favour). We need God's pardon (penalty removed for what we've done) so that we may start over. This is accomplished by simply turning from our way of doing things and from our way of thinking and returning to the Lord. Reformers Unanimous is here to show you how to do this. I hope you listen to what God has to say to you. God bless.

❖ **Accept the blames for your actions, and God will remove the guilt.**

As a young man trying to get away from the strongholds of my addictions, I sought the counsel and help of people in secular programs. Time and time again, they searched for hidden meaning in my behaviour. They explained how my rebellion and desire to please myself was most assuredly to be blamed on my parents, that I had been forced into my sin by what they referred to as bad surroundings. Many in society today are teaching us to shift the blame for our shortcomings on our parents, our upbringing, our economic background, our race, our minority status, and many other things. By shifting the blame to others, it temporarily removes the guilt.

You see, God designed us with a spiritual equilibrium. When we commit sin, we experience guilt, and it throws our spirit off balance with our emotions.

When society teaches us to shift the blame, or if we naturally shift the blame, we actually can circumvent that off-balance feeling of guilt temporarily. However, when the sin returns, the guilt is so much worse. Our feelings of failure increase to even higher levels. God's design is to administer guilt through His spirit that lives within the believer. That guilt needs to be released, and God designed a formula for that to happen.

> **If we confess our sins, He is faithful and just to forgive us our sins, and to cleanse us from all unrighteousness. (1 John 1:9)**

What a beautiful promise! *If*, a big word. If we do, He will. If we don't, He won't.

If we confess (proclaim to God) our sin, He is faithful (for sure, 100 percent of the time, over and over) to forgive (full pardon) our sins. He doesn't stop there. You see, we have been pardoned for our wrongdoing, but we are not cleaned from it. We still have the guilty feeling. We must be cleansed of all unrighteousness. If my daughter got dressed for Sunday school and then went outside and fell in the mud, I would not only forgive her for playing outside when it was raining and she was dressed for Sunday school. I would also clean her. I would give her a bath and all new clothes. Why? Because when I bring her to Sunday school, I don't want anyone to know that she fell in the mud. That is what God wants to do for us. He wants to give us a full pardon for everything we've done in the past, and He wants to clean us up and put us in a new set of clothes. And He is faithful. That means He wants to do this every time we sin against Him. He loves us that much. So today, accept the blame for what you have done in your life. Confess it to God, and He will clean you up. Praise God!

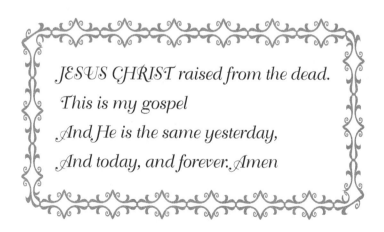

JESUS CHRIST raised from the dead.

This is my gospel

And He is the same yesterday,

And today, and forever. Amen

CHAPTER

The Power of Man Over Darkness

Darkness in this contest is not the mere absence of light to see things around us or to read our books in the house but principalities and evil rulers in high places that often contend with man. Darkness is the comprehensiveness of evils and diseases, storms and tribulations that man daily encounters as he lives on earth. When we talk about darkness, we mean forces that rise against our glorious and fruitful life.

Man was given the power to overcome diseases and to live a healthy life.

These powers live as darkness around us and also use dark places, like evil altars, throne, covens, and shrines to cover up, to build satanic plans and develop wicked arrows against man, and to manipulate man's mind into doing things that ordinarily man wouldn't have done against himself or God; that afflicted man and caused him to lose faith in God.

In every house you can see around, in every home, in every city or town or village, there are powers of darkness that pull and push man from the salvation race and wickedly rule man and twist his life into wrongdoings and choose sins instead of holiness.

In all these, man was created by a powerful and a mighty God, whose name is I Am that I Am, the Almighty Jehovah, the light in the darkness, the unquestionable God, the Alpha and Omega. His powers are unlimited, and with the same power, man was created. Man became as powerful as his Creator because all powers were given unto him to rule over everything. That includes living and nonliving things, visible and invisible. Man is god on earth, and everything on earth are placed under the authority of man's leadership.

> **Behold, I give unto you power to tread on serpents and scorpions, and over all the power of the enemy: and nothing shall by any means hurt you. (Luke 10:10, KJV)**

This power that we have through Jesus Christ was the same power that raised Him from the grave and defeated death and the devil completely. Jesus Christ ordained us with God's power, and man became a carrier of supernatural powers that crush the devil and set ablaze its powers. Man has no reason to fear any power, visible or invisible.

> **Let every soul be subject unto the higher powers. For there is no power but of God: the powers that be are ordained of God. (Romans 13:1, KJV)**

> **[18]Then Jesus came to them and said, 'All authority in heaven and on earth has been given to me. [19]Therefore go and make disciples of all nations, baptizing them in the name of the Father and of the Son and of the Holy Spirit, [20]and teaching them to obey everything I have commanded you. And surely I am with you always, to the very end of the age. (Matthew 28:18–20, NIV)**

Promise made and promised kept: 'Surely I am with you always'. There is no power of enemies that can face man and that will overcome him. This secret is important for every Christian to know, that Lucifer and his agents have been defeated and you are more powerful than any witches or wizards or any evil powers you can imagine.

> **What then shall we say to these things? If God *is* for us, who *can be* against us? (Romans 8:31, NKJV)**

The powers of darkness know that God loves us and He is ready to do anything for us. He made us powerful than the angels in heaven; at our command, the angels are released into battle. Our Lord Jesus Christ has given the believers power to do the works He did, and even greater works. (John 14: 12, Luke 10:19)

No evil power can withstand or resist your God-given power.

Lucifer, the leader of all evil powers and ruler of darkness, knows that the children of God have the power to overcome him completely. Not to talk of stupid powers like demons, witches, and evil spirits, or have you ever seen where light bows down before darkness? Light destroys all darkness.

The word of God actually called us light. I am light, and no power of darkness dares me.

You are the light of the world. A town built on a hill cannot be hidden. (Matthew 5:14, NIV)

Listen to me: Don't allow any man to deceive you that you cannot defeat the devil.

You are *light* and created to shine and magnify God. The only reason why you can lose the battle to the devil temporarily is when you are hidden from heavenly powers by sin. It is difficult for light to be hidden. Anywhere light is darkness is hidden or cannot be seen.

Anywhere I pass, no darkness or evil power stands on my path; for it was scripturally commanded upon me and my spiritual duty to cast out all demons and to rule over powers and principalities and to shine to the glory of His Father in heaven.

When I hear some faithless or half-baked Christians running from pillar to post, looking for cover or powers to defeat the devil, I often wonder, do they really understand what they read in the Bible? How can you defeat what you have already defeated? Or how can you run away from a lifeless dead snake? Lucifer is powerless. There's no life in him. Christians have the life of Jesus Christ, and they live by Christ's life. Whatever you had overcome can never overcome you.

Your question is, 'Pastor, why are Christians still praying to overcome evil powers of Lucifer?'

Answer: Not everyone who goes to church is genuinely born again with heavenly powers to overcome all forces of evil because some people find it difficult to flee away from all appearances of evil or sin. The devil knows those he cannot mess up with. Sin is the reason for our struggles in life and continuous battles with the powers of darkness.

But fear not. God has given us victory over the devil through the name of Jesus Christ.

> **Behold, I give unto you power to tread on serpents and scorpions, and over all the power of the enemy: and nothing shall by any means hurt you. (Luke 10:19, KJV)**

> **Ye are of God, little children, and have overcome them: because greater is he that is in you, than he that is in the world. (1 John 4:4, KJV)**

Tell the devil to get lost. Flush him out of your life into the gutters mercilessly.

Flush him out of your womb as a woman, and as a man, kick the devil out of your dreams, out of your family, and out of your environment permanently. Greater is He who is in us than the Lucifer in this world. You are of God, so never take no for an answer from the devil or from any man. If the devil says no, that you cannot be healed of your temporary sickness, tell him to get lost. You are healthy and bouncing in the Lord. You are healed by His stripes.

Haven't you heard that all powers are ordained by God and nothing shall by any means hurt you? If the devil cannot hurt God, he can't hurt you also. If you are born of God, you are born of victorious powers, and in you are blessings of God and nothing can stop you. This is our hope in him:

> **For whatsoever is born of God overcometh the world: and this is the victory that overcometh the world, even our faith. (1 John 5:4, KJV)**

Satan, get lost in my life and marriage. I command you to get lost right away in my business, in my health, in my children, and in my ministry. I say get lost in Jesus's name. Amen. Praise God!

Three facts you must understand if you want to end life struggles:

1. Stay alert. There's an enemy.

Be alert and of sober mind. Your enemy, the devil, prowls around like a roaring lion looking for someone to devour. (1 Peter 5:8, NIV)

There are forces that move around for four things:

i.   To gather information about you and report to principalities and powers. I call them evil spiritual journalists.

ii. To devour or cause pain to innocents.

iii. To barricade the innocent's path with gates of irons and bars and cobwebs.

iv. To set traps and dig pits for the innocents.

Stay alert in prayers and fasting because the enemies are not sleeping and are not ready to sleep, so you must not sleep either.

There two kinds of species of this animal – enemies:

a. Crepuscular species, such as tigers, rabbits, and skunks; hyenas are often referred to as nocturnal animals.
b. Cathemeral species, such as fossae and lions, are active in the day and night.

When you have these animals, like tigers and lions, around you as enemies that refuse to sleep and wouldn't allow you to sleep, you must make their lairs unsettled. Set all midnight powers ablaze and command them buried alive. Suffer not a witch to live. Chase them out of covens every midnight through dangerous prayers. Let the legs of every witch tormenting me swell up with sores and die in Jesus's name. Dangerous problems require dangerous prayer at midnight.

Stay awake at night if you want to be successful in life and live a complete problem-free life. This evil species of wickedness never sleep until they kill the innocents. Child of God, listen to me, get the sword of God and kill these evil species out of your life. The roaring lions and flesh-eating tigers, kill them, I say!

2. Don't be ignorant of Satan.

Lest Satan should take advantage of us, for we are not ignorant of his devices.

2 Corinthians 2:11

When you get advantage over something, you can conquer the thing. You can only be taken advantage of when you are ignorant of the devil's devices. The devil will not attack you until he knows that

i.   you are ignorant of his devices,
ii.   you are careless with sins,
iii. you are not as prayerful as before,
iv.   when he has fully understood your weakness, and
v.   when he has taken advantage of you.

Christians must be smart and quick to attack their attackers spiritually through fasting and prayers. Don't cheaply accept storms of life as normal. Rise in prayer and fight back and regain your freedom. Stand your ground and deploy all weapons of war against the devices of the devil.

3. The evil one can't touch you.

We know that whosoever is born of God sinneth not; but he that is begotten of God keepeth himself, and that wicked one toucheth him not. (1 John 5:18)

From now on let no one trouble me, for I bear in my body the marks of the LORD Jesus. (Galatians 6:17, NKJV)

No evil person can trouble you because there are a marks of 'trouble not my anointed', and if they make an attempt, God rewards such evil one with death.

The very day I read this scripture, I knew immediately that no one can touch, trouble, or speak evil against me without God punishing the person with disasters and death.

If you really know that you have our Lord Jesus Christ's marks in your body, don't be afraid of witchcraft marks or evil marks. No evil marks can survive in your body, for your body is covered with the marks of Jesus Christ, and His marks are more powerful than any evil marks.

When you get hold of the word of God in your spirit, release the weapons of victory on your frustrations and storms of life. Stop the devil's mouth from eating your blessings and let him know that you are untouchable.

> **There is no divination against Jacob, no evil omens against Israel. It will now be said of Jacob and of Israel, 'See what God has done!' (Numbers 23:23, NIV)**

I called you child of powers. That's what you are. Rise and start looking for the enemy of your destiny or the reason behind your problems and destroy it.

God has developed deadly and massively-destructive weapons the world can never withstand or contend with. You must use the deadly, powerful weapon now against Lucifer, witches, and all powers of darkness.

I am the begotten of God, and nothing can touch me. Be aggressive in your prayers and pray in the spirit to terminate all unfavourable situations that raise its head against you.

> **'No weapon formed against you shall prosper, and every tongue *which* rises against**

you in judgment you shall condemn. This
***is* the heritage of the servants of the LORD,**
and their righteousness *is* from Me', says the
LORD. (Isaiah 54:17, NKJV)

No weapon has the capability to destroy a child of God. All man-made weapons are subject to weakness. The only supernatural and undefeated weapon is the word of God. There is no one who goes into battle with the word of God and gets disappointed. Anyone who puts up a fight against the anointed gets defeated by the anointed power of the word of God. 'By the anointing, every yoke must be broken'.

The servants of God have exclusive battle-ready powers at their command.

These powers are fearful to Lucifer himself and never underestimates their potential.

If you want God to declare war against you, touch His anointed ones. There was a time in my ministry in a city called Ancona in Italy when God made me a great fear to all witches and wizards. Every activity of powers of darkness in the land was set ablaze. This city is a citadel of evil powers in Italy.

In one of our Sunday services, as I finished ministration, a woman walked to me at the pulpit and said, 'Man of God, I was sent from the witches' meeting today to attend your service and see the power you have and why I wouldn't let them be'.

I told her, 'Madam, go and tell the witches in this city to pack out of this city or start to repent. Otherwise, they will start to die one by one'.

She then left the altar of God and went away.

Who is like my God? I will not fear any power, and any power that wants to touch me shall die in Jesus's name.

Child of God, do you know that in the city of Ancona, Italy, God proved to my enemies that I am His servant and no weapon formed against me shall prosper.

When you release your faith in prayer, He releases His powerful weapons quick and fast at your command. People thought that my voice will not be heard again, but God distributed problems upon everyone who troubled me, my family, and my ministry. Some are still in deep trouble till this day.

Witches and wizards are denied sleep, happiness, everything. My God spoiled all their labour.

I pray for everyone who is reading my book that God shall send thunder and unquenchable fires upon territorial witchcrafts in Jesus's name. Amen.

Christians' Power over Darkness

❖ **Greater is He that is in you.**

> **Ye are of God, little children, and have overcome them: because greater is he that is in you, than he that is in the world. (1 John 4:4, KJV)**

There is a greater He in you that even the greatest power of darkness can never withstand. He is the I Am that I Am, the Almighty God, the Creator of all things, and the beginning of all things in heaven, on earth, and under the earth. He is stronger than the strongest. His powers are incomparable and undefeatable. All powers bow at the mention of His name. When His own calls unto Him, He answers them.

Never you see yourself as powerless before any challenges. You are given powers that no human or spiritual powers can overcome. The specimens to terminate all powers of darkness is the blood of Jesus Christ. It's true that in the world, there are powers of darkness and principalities that cause pains and afflictions.

Hear this: The fact that you live in this wicked world does not mean that your life depends on the world.

If you are born of God, you need not be afraid of the lesser powers. You must always display the power of 'the greater' in you and never accept options from the lesser in the world.

Until you are wrapped with greater grace, disgrace will make you look lesser in this world. Only those who are surrounded with the power of God see other powers of darkness as non-issues. To satisfy God's requirement of admission into His kingdom, you must fight powers of darkness stand still. You must fight to overcome.

Then you will be called a man of war like your Heavenly Father.

God's children are greater than any powers, visible or invisible, and never fall for intimidations of midnight powers. Smoke them out of their covens with dangerous prayer from midnight to 3:30 a.m.

When I was not yet born again, I was denied sleep and no rest of mind. There is no month that I will not be knocked down with pains and sickness. But when I met 'the greater' than the greatest, I took sleep out of the eyes of witches and wizards, withheld their peace, made witches look panicking at all night through the sound of my voice calling the Holy Ghost's fires upon witches' heads and covens to catch fire. Even Lucifer never slept or drank a cup of tea with peace again. I am their greatest nightmare. 'The greater' in me is the fear of Lucifer and his agents. I fear no man or powers in Jesus's name.

❖ **You have overcome the world.**

For whatsoever is born of God overcometh the world: and this is the victory that overcometh the world, even our faith. (1 John 5:4, KJV)

Overcoming the world is your spiritual homework, and your sole faith grants you victory. The day you are born again, you overcometh the world. If God is not afraid of the world He created, why are you afraid of the world that your Father created?

The earth is of the Lord's and the fullness thereof, the world and they that dwell in it. Everything in this world are mandated by God to obey His command.

We are not asked to fear the world we live in, but we are commanded by God that we should go into the world and multiply, subdue, and occupy everything, leaving nothing for the devil to enjoy. We are to chase Lucifer out of hiding places and send him to the pit of hell.

Anything you overcame cannot overcome you. In the spiritual classroom, Satan cannot undo what giants in faith have done. There are multitudes of angels in heaven that are ready for deployment into war zones in your life. They are only waiting for your command. Subdue the world and make God proud. That is what God wants to see in our spiritual report card. Put your faith to work and crush all powers of darkness. Hear this: You cannot overcome when you are a friend to the world.

Step out of the darkness and accept Jesus Christ, then the power to overcome the world will be released upon you.

❖ **You have overcome the evil one.**

> **I write unto you, fathers, because ye have known him that is from the beginning. I write unto you, young men, because ye have overcome the wicked one. I write unto you, little children, because ye have known the Father. (1 John 2:13, KJV)**

The greatest power to overcome the world is 'knowing the Father' through His Son Jesus Christ. There is no evil that can touch you or be near your dwelling place. Those who know the Son and the Father, the world knows them with uncommon results. Do you know that witches and wicked people know Lucifer and they also know that his powers are defeatable? How do you serve God without knowing His powers, what He is capable of doing, and what He asks you to do? Go ye into the world and spread His name (gospel), cast out devils, overcome all forces of darkness. He that is in you and working in you and through you will confirm your words with signs and wonders. Evil fears signs and wonders that are beyond their little powers or imaginations. Who told you to be afraid of evil people or midnight powers of darkness? Are they as strong as you are? Can they match you in authority and powers? Or can their god be like our God? Their rock is not like our Rock.

[31] For their rock is not as our Rock, even our enemies themselves being judges. Deuteronomy 32:31(KJV)

Who is their creator? No one. But we have a Creator—I Am that I Am, Almighty Jehovah. Goliath met Him in David's life, and the battle was too tough to withstand. Goliath was unable to overcome David's small stone and catapult. David effortlessly cut off his head. The lions saw the Almighty God in Daniel's life and they could not think of eating flesh again. Daniel overcome lion's death.

[16] Then the king commanded, and they brought Daniel, and cast him into the den of lions. Now the king spake and said unto Daniel, Thy God whom thou servest continually, he will deliver thee.

[17] And a stone was brought, and laid upon the mouth of the den; and the king sealed it with his own signet, and with the signet of his lords; that the purpose might not be changed concerning Daniel.

[18] Then the king went to his palace, and passed the night fasting: neither were instruments of musick brought before him: and his sleep went from him.

[19] Then the king arose very early in the morning, and went in haste unto the den of lions.

[20] And when he came to the den, he cried with a lamentable voice unto Daniel: and the king spake and said to Daniel, O Daniel, servant of

the living God, is thy God, whom thou servest continually, able to deliver thee from the lions?

[21] Then said Daniel unto the king, O king, live for ever.

[22] My God hath sent his angel, and hath shut the lions' mouths, that they have not hurt me: forasmuch as before him innocency was found in me; and also before thee, O king, have I done no hurt. Daniel 6: 16- 22 (KJV)

Men of faith display their supernatural powers and make a public show of all powers of the devil.

Since you know the Father and the Son, and They know you, consider everything done at your command. There is spiritual covering over your life that evil ones cannot overcome. You are a product of the mighty power that created the whole world; other powers dare you not. Your weapon is not earthly-made but heavenly-developed to pull down strong holds and forces of darkness.

❖ **Stand firm in faith.**

Resist him, standing firm in the faith, because you know that the family of believers throughout the world is undergoing the same kind of sufferings. (1 Peter 5:9, NIV)

What makes a strong man lose a battle is when he sees your firm stand to resist him. Be firm in your faith. Never be moved even in a worse situation. Let your faith speak for you on the day of powers display. The prophet Elijah's faith in

God spoke for him before his enemies when he displayed the power of God. The fire leaked all waters, and the enemies were greatly amazed.

Get the enemy down right away, keep them off your environment, never allow them to live, and cut off their sources of powers.

You can't say you have faith in God and still refuse to set ablaze all powers of darkness. 'Suffered not a witch to live'. Stand firm in faith like David against any Goliath and cut off the throat of your enemies with their own sword.

Fear will not only defeat you but also lead you to your early death. Warriors are never afraid of their opponent; neither do warriors drop their swords to their enemies cheaply. You are a warrior, and God's word in your mouth is your sword. The devil fears the word of God and respects those who speak the words of God in faith.

Until your enemies see you as danger to their existence, they will always deny your existence. Christians are the ones permitting the evil one to live around them and stay in their marriage and business. When you take a firm stand, the enemy will never be willing to hear your name or be willing to poke nose on your affairs again.

Be as powerful as the word of God. Conquering the enemy is a non-issue.

You don't need to have sleepless nights for witchcraft or voodoo powers. All that is required of you is to know God the Father. Your faith can place the devil in a situation he can never recover from forever. Moses's faith in God placed Egypt in a weeping and sad situation till this day. Your faith will not be respected until it does dangerous and amazing things. Faith will only be called faith when enemies are afraid to attack you. Ignite the fire of your faith, and the fire of your enemies will stop.

Great men of faith overcome great enemies, and those who stand firm in faith never fall for enemies to laugh. You need no legs to stand firm in this world because of the way the world is going, but you need faith as legs to stand against the devil and its power that is ruling the world. It's your faith that called you a child of God, not the church you attended. Therefore, stand firm on your faith at all times till our Lord Jesus returns.

DANGEROUS PRAYERS TO OVERCOME ALL DARK POWERS

There is no problem or evil powers that the word of God cannot defeat. The word of God is superior to all powers, that includes evil authorities, principalities, and thrones.

Those who throw away their faith, fasting life, and prayer belt have obliged to defeat.

Four things are important when you want to overcome all enemies of your life:

a. You must have the desire to pray.
b. You must create a quite environment to pray and not a noisy place.
c. You must have the spirit of prayer.
d. You must pray with faith and hope.

This kind of prayers are best prayed at midnight for effective results.

Though some enemies strike or send evil arrows in the daytime, you can pray in the day, but remember that at midnight, all evil spirits, dead spirits, come out at night to operate. Wicked and harmful powers by witchdoctors are also lose and tried on people. The most important thing is that you must apply the four rules above to cause disasters upon your enemies either in the day or at night. Give enemies no time to strike you but destroy them completely and pull down their habitations.

It is important you confess Jesus Christ as your Lord and Saviour, and be born again, then you have the full backing of host angels to destroy all evil powers.

Read Numbers 23:23, Psalms 7:15–16, Psalms 9:5, Psalms 11:6, and Jeremiah 30:16–17.

Sing praises and worship songs. Cover yourself and every property with the blood of Jesus Christ.

1. Arrows of insanity fired into my spirit, backfire in the name of Jesus.
2. Arrows of untimely death fired into my dream life, backfire in the name of Jesus.
3. Occultist arrows fired into my health, come out and backfire to sender in the name of Jesus.
4. Witchcraft arrows of discouragement fired into my spirit, backfire in the name of Jesus.
5. Witchcraft involvement in my business, marriage, my health challenges, etc., thunder fire of God's words, arise and destroy them and let them die in Jesus's name.

6. Arrows of barrenness fired into my womb and genitals, backfire in the name of Jesus.
7. Arrows and curses of non-achievement fired into my destiny, backfire in the name of Jesus.
8. Judgement of darkness, witches, or evil people upon my name, backfire in the name of Jesus.
9. Satanic carpenters building coffin for me, enter your coffin and die in the name of Jesus.
10. Environmental pharaoh that holds me captive, release me and die by fire in the name of Jesus.
11. Arrows fired by the queen of the seas into my life or ministry or marriage, backfire in the name of Jesus.
12. Arrows of automatic failure fired against my life, backfire in the name of Jesus.
13. Every evil arrow of sudden tragedy fired into my life, backfire in the name of Jesus.
14. Cloud of darkness around my breakthroughs, scatter in the name of Jesus.
15. Every evil padlock holding down my progress, open by fire and release my progress in the name of Jesus.
16. Wind of the spirit, carry me to my destination in the name of Jesus.
17. Blessings from unexpected quarters, locate me by fire in the name of Jesus.
18. Evil covenant of hard labour of my father's house that is affecting my life, be broken in the name of Jesus.
19. Satan's installations against your life and destiny, be destroyed in Jesus's name.
20. Oh, God, heap disasters upon my enemies and shoot them down with your arrows in Jesus's name. (Deuteronomy 32:23)
21. Oh, God, cut off all witchcraft legs standing on my progress and destiny in Jesus's name. Amen.

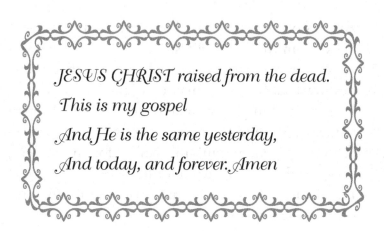

JESUS CHRIST raised from the dead.

This is my gospel

And He is the same yesterday,

And today, and forever. Amen

OTHER BOOKS BY THE AUTHOR

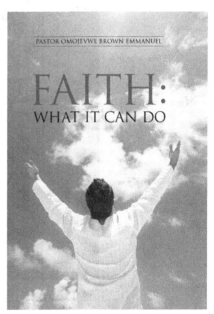

The Wound of Humanity   Faith: What It Can Do

The Devil Must Fear Your Name

ABOUT THE AUTHOR

I was a great sinner, committing all kinds of atrocities. I never went to church, and I was a womaniser and blasphemer of the gospel of Jesus Christ. Now I found grace, repentance, forgiveness, and perfection. I am prepared by grace, honoured, qualified, chosen, accepted, and cleansed by the blood of Jesus—I am a preacher of the gospel I once condemned.

Pastor Emmanuel Brown Omojevwe is the founder and general overseer of True Vine Evangelical Bible Ministry worldwide. He is based in Italy, where the headquarters of the church is found. He is a prophet, teacher, evangelist, pastor, preacher, prolific writer, poet, and international public speaker. He is a man whom God is using all over Europe to anoint, deliver, and bring transformations to millions. He is a husband and a father to millions, a humble man of God who believes that God can use anyone irrespective of his or her sins, circumstances, and backgrounds as long he or she is pruned by God.

His desire is to preach the gospel of Christ to all nations so that peace could be obtained and the body of Christ is united. Also, he is of the opinion that materialism gospel should not be a focal point of a true man of God

Printed in the United States
by Baker & Taylor Publisher Services